Praise for *Cooking at the Academy*

"Best of the Year: The hottest and most savory TV cooking show is produced by San Francisco's California Culinary Academy and KQED. The series...features no-name, no-frills chefs who skip yuks and patter in favor of precise instructions on how to concoct their...au courant recipes."

—Time Magazine

Awarded four toques. *"If you can't take a cooking class, the Academy is the next best thing....No bad puns, burnt meringues, or other goofy gaffes."*

—Cox News Service

"It is skillfully done,...carefully paced and instructive."

—Washington Post

"If you want to learn to cook or have yearned to attend a professional cooking school, you'll enjoy Cooking at the Academy....*Personable chef-instructors demystify fundamental cooking techniques."*

—Houston Chronicle

"This is the kind of cookbook that one can thumb through and be tantalized by many of the recipes....Absolutely mouth-watering."

—Palo Alto Weekly

*"The series promotes cooking for its own sake....Viewers learn cooking techniques needed to get them through most sticky culinary situations....*Cooking at the Academy *takes the focus off the individual and places it back where it belongs: on cooking."*

—National Culinary Review

*"*Cooking at the Academy *has become a delicious success."*

—San Francisco Chronicle

Companion to the Public Television Series
Cooking at the Academy

FESTIVE FAVORITES

—

*Entertaining with the
California Culinary Academy*

Cooking at the Academy is made possible by generous grants from

Wästhof-Trident Cutlery

Circulon Commercial

Everpure, Inc.

Chicago Metallic

KQED
BOOKS

SAN FRANCISCO

The dessert recipes on pages 120, 138, 148, 154, 160, and 197 are adapted from *The Professional Pastry Chef* by Bo Friberg, © 1995, published by Van Nostrand Reinhold, and used with permission.

For KQED:
President and CEO: Mary G. F. Bitterman
Vice President for Publishing and New Ventures: Mark K. Powelson

For the California Culinary Academy:
President and CEO: Alexander M. Hehmeyer
Director — Media: David Chomsky

Publisher: Pamela Byers
Production Coordinator and Editor: Zipporah W. Collins
Art Direction: Adrian Morgan
Design: Kristin Becktsoffer
CCA Liaisons: Johnathan Robinette, Jurgen Weise, CMC
Photographer: Robert Olding
Photography Food and Prop Stylist: Denise Vivaldo
Photography Chef: Carl Abbott
(The desserts shown in the photos on the cover and on pages 121, 139, 149, 155, and 161 were prepared and styled by Bo Friberg.)
Acknowledgment for props provided for the photographs is on page 214

Educational and nonprofit groups wishing to order this book at attractive quantity discounts may contact KQED Books and Tapes, 2601 Mariposa Street, San Francisco, CA 94110.

Library of Congress Cataloging-in-Publication Data
Festive favorites : entertaining with the California Culinary Academy.
　　　p.　cm.
　　"Companion to the public television series Cooking at the Academy."
　　Includes index.
　　ISBN 0−912333−12−X
　　1. Cookery.　　2. Entertaining.　　I. California Culinary Academy.　　II. Cooking at the Academy (Television program)
TX714.F47　1995
614.5 — dc20   95−52
                                                                          CIP

ISBN 0−912333−12−X
Manufactured in the United States of America
10　9　8　7　6　5　4　3　2　1

On the cover: *Crème Caramel Nouvelle* (see page 138)

Distributed to the trade by Publishers Group West

CONTENTS

Starters   23

Starters

Entrées   61

Breads

Sauces Stocks & Gifts

Et Cetera

Introduction

٭

This cookbook is your guide to entertaining with the flair, flash, and finesse of a team of professional chefs. It contains over 125 recipes developed by the talented chef / instructors and alumni of the California Culinary Academy—recipes designed especially for use in the home kitchen. Wherever possible, ease of preparation and respect for the time constraints of today's busy lifestyles make these recipes as practical as they are delicious and impressive. Representing over 150 years of culinary expertise, this stunning recipe collection reflects California Culinary Academy style—creative use of ingredients, time-saving techniques, and presentations developed with the understanding that taste begins with the eye.

As the twenty-first century approaches and technology seems to advance faster than the speed of light, we are witnessing a renewed emphasis on home. A refuge from the pressures of the outside world, a respite from life's hectic pace, home is today's oasis. A desire to share that peaceful oasis with family and friends has brought interest in home entertaining to the forefront, and, since time immemorial, food has been the symbol of hospitality. The second season of the television series *Cooking at the Academy* focuses on new and traditional ways to offer that hospitality.

In the first season, California Culinary Academy chef / instructors demonstrated basic cooking techniques that form the foundation for all cuisines. This focus on techniques mirrors the Academy's philosophy of culinary education, which emphasizes the fundamentals of modern classical cooking and baking, while developing a heightened awareness of the senses. With the second season, *Cooking at the Academy* incorporates those techniques into a style of entertaining that will distinguish your gatherings from all others.

Happy Entertaining!

Alexander M. Hehmeyer

President and CEO

Jurgen Weise

Certified Master Chef

About the Chefs

Dan Bowe Culinary educator, food stylist, catering expert, and food writer are a few of the hats that fit this versatile culinarian. A 1984 graduate of the California Culinary Academy and 1990 graduate of the School for American Chefs, directed by Madeleine Kamman at Beringer Vineyards, Chef Bowe was the founder of Cuisine Cuisine, a catering and events production business in San Francisco. In 1990, he returned to the Academy as a member of the faculty, teaching catering and kitchen management for four years. He currently teaches courses for cooking enthusiasts through the Academy's consumer education department.

Linda Carucci Chef Carucci was an educator prior to becoming a chef. Upon graduation from the California Culinary Academy in 1984, she spent several years in the foodservice industry before returning in 1989 to become the dean of students of the Academy, combining her education and culinary careers. She is the author of *California Chefs Cook LEAN*, published by California Project LEAN. Chef Carucci is currently a culinary arts consultant, teaching cooking to children and adults.

Tamara Frey A 1979 graduate of the California Culinary Academy, Chef Frey runs a successful catering business and is active in the family-owned Frey Vineyards, a leading producer of premium organic wines. Chef Frey was an executive chef at The Daily Planet, a popular bistro in Burlington, Vermont, has had numerous recipes published, and designed and directed the Kitchen Garden Cooking School, featuring her unique style of vegetarian spa cuisine, at the world-renowned resort spa Rancho La Puerta in Tecate, Mexico.

Bo Friberg Chef Friberg is a pastry chef/instructor at the California Culinary Academy. He is a graduate of the Confectionary Association School of Sweden and holds a degree as a Certified Master Pastry Chef. He has worked in restaurants and pastry shops in Sweden and the United States and was pastry chef for Swedish American Lines Cruise Ships. Chef Friberg has received Swedish and U.S. honors for his work, including two gold medals at the American Culinary Federation Culinary Arts Exhibit of the Pacific Coast. He is the author of *The Professional Pastry Chef*, second edition and forthcoming third edition, an 800-page pastry and baking compendium. Chef Friberg also appeared in the first season of *Cooking at the Academy*.

Louie Jocson Shortly after graduation from the California Culinary Academy in 1990, Chef Jocson joined the culinary staff of Antonello Ristorante, a five-star restaurant in Southern California, and soon rose to the title of sous chef. In March 1994, he was promoted once again and is currently the pastry chef of both Antonello Ristorante and Antonello Espresso Bar. In addition, Chef Jocson has built a personal following from creating exclusive dining adventures in private homes.

Michael Kalanty Chef Kalanty is a chef/instructor in the California Culinary Academy's baking and pastry program and a member of the American Culinary Federation. He was awarded a scholarship to the School for American Chefs, directed by Madeleine Kamman at Beringer Vineyards. After receiving pastry training at Pâtisserie Pomme d'Api in Chambly, France, Chef Kalanty taught a professional pastry chef program in his native Philadelphia and cofounded Video-Chef, Inc., an instructional video production company. In addition to his professional classes, Chef Kalanty teaches nonprofessionals through the consumer education department of the California Culinary Academy.

Lars Kronmark Chef Kronmark is one of the California Culinary Academy's most senior chef/instructors. A native of Denmark, he graduated from the Restaurant and Hotel Apprenticeship School of Copenhagen. He worked in several restaurants and resorts in England, Denmark, and Switzerland, including the Hôtel de la Paix in Geneva, before joining the California Culinary Academy in 1981. Chef Kronmark has taught a wide variety of subjects to students at all levels in the Academy, from freshman to senior class. In 1987, he participated in a culinary exchange program with Adelaide Regency College in southern Australia.

Teresa Douglas/Mitchell Chef Mitchell graduated with outstanding merit from the California Culinary Academy in 1987. Currently the culinary director for Korbel Champagne Cellars, Chef Mitchell has been associated with San Francisco's Campton Place hotel and the Vintners Inn in Sonoma County, California. She was owner/operator and executive chef at the Half Shell Restaurant in San Francisco for three years. She has made television appearances around the country, and has contributed to such publications as *Victoria Magazine, Chef's Magazine,* the Gannett Group, and the *San Francisco Chronicle.*

Johnathan Robinette   Formerly director of culinary education and executive chef, Johnathan Robinette was with the California Culinary Academy for five years. During his tenure, he was responsible for all aspects of culinary education, including development of curriculum guidelines and standards, culinary research and development, and supervision and professional development of chef/instructors. Chef Robinette was technical adviser for *Cooking at the Academy's* first season and coauthored the companion cookbook. A contributing editor to the *National Culinary Review*, he was awarded the magazine's Henry Award for best technique article in both 1993 and 1994.

Greg Tompkins   A 1986 graduate of the California Culinary Academy, Chef Tompkins is the Director of Culinary Operations for Just Desserts/Tassajara Bread Bakery in San Francisco, which is widely acknowledged to have sparked the current resurgence of artisanal bread making in the United States. Prior to joining Just Desserts, Chef Tompkins was a pastry chef/instructor on the faculty of the California Culinary Academy, and he continues to teach courses in the Academy's consumer education department. Chef Tompkins also appeared in the first season of *Cooking at the Academy*.

Breakfasts and Brunches

✴

Sticky Bun Pull-Aparts

Greg Tompkins

The sweet milk dough used for these buns is fine for a great number of breakfast pastries.
See the cinnamon roll variation following this recipe for an example.

Serves 6

1 1/4 cups milk

6 tablespoons soft butter

3/4 teaspoons granulated sugar

3/4 teaspoon salt

1 egg, lightly beaten

About 4 cups all-purpose flour

1 package rapid-rise yeast

1 1/2 cups loose brown sugar

1/2 cup dark corn syrup

3/4 cup coarsely chopped pecans

3/4 cup raisins

2 teaspoons ground cinnamon

1. In a medium saucepan, heat the milk to scalding. Add 2 tablespoons of the butter, the sugar, and the salt, and stir, off the heat, until the butter has melted and the sugar and salt have dissolved.

2. Let the mixture cool enough so that it won't cook the egg. Then beat in the egg. Set aside.

3. In a large mixer bowl, combine 2 cups of the flour and the yeast. Stir to blend.

4. Pour in the milk mixture, and beat with a paddle until the batter is smooth.

5. Switch to a dough hook, and add 1 3/4 cups of the remaining flour. Knead at low speed until the flour is moistened, then knead at medium speed about 8 minutes, until the dough is smooth and soft. Add the remaining flour if necessary to form the dough into a ball.

6. Place the dough in a lightly oiled bowl, cover the bowl with plastic wrap, and allow the dough to proof in a warm place until doubled in size.

7. While the dough is rising, make the sticky mix. Combine the remaining butter, 3/4 cup of the brown sugar, and the corn syrup in a heavy saucepan, and heat over a low flame for 5 minutes, until the mixture is smooth. Divide the mixture evenly between 2 9-inch Bundt pans. Sprinkle the chopped pecans equally over the bottoms of the pans.

8. After the dough has doubled, roll it on a lightly floured surface into a 10-by-18-inch rectangle. Press the raisins into the dough.

9. In a small bowl, stir together the remaining 3/4 cup of brown sugar and the cinnamon. Sprinkle the mixture evenly over the dough.

10. Beginning with the long side of the dough rectangle, roll the dough up like a jelly roll. Cut the roll crosswise into 12 equal pieces. Place 6 slices, cut side down, in each Bundt pan.

11. Heat the oven to 350°F while you allow the buns to rise until doubled. Bake them for 25 to 30 minutes. As each pan comes from the oven, immediately invert it onto a serving plate. Serve warm (but not hot from the oven). *

Variation: Cinnamon Rolls

Increase the raisins and brown sugar to 1 cup each and the cinnamon to 1 tablespoon. Press 3 tablespoons of cold butter slivers into the dough with the raisins in step 8.

Fruit and Cream Scones

Greg Tompkins

Any dried fruit may be used in these scones, either singly or a mix. Given the blandness of the scone dough, however, an acid fruit (such as dried apricots or sour cherries) produces a superior product. The dough will also benefit from the addition of spices. Try prune scones with $1/3$ teaspoon of ground cardamom, or fig scones with $1/2$ teaspoon of ground anise seed.

It is not necessary to soak the fruit at length. Covering it briefly with water starts the rehydration process, and the drained fruit will continue to absorb water that remains on its skin. The object is not to completely rehydrate the fruit but to soften it slightly and make it more toothsome.

Serves 16

1 cup dried fruit (one kind or a mixture, such as apricots, raisins, and cranberries)

$5 1/2$ cups pastry flour

$1/2$ cup sugar

2 tablespoons baking powder

1 teaspoon salt

$2 1/2$ cups heavy cream, plus 4 tablespoons (for brushing)

About 3 tablespoons AA (coarse granulated) sugar (for sprinkling)

1. Cover the fruit mixture with cool water for 1 minute to soften it slightly. Break apart any lumps of fruit that are stuck together. Drain the fruit and set it aside.

2. In a 5-quart mixer bowl, combine the flour, sugar, baking powder, and salt, and stir to blend well. Add the 2½ cups of cream, then the fruit.

3. Blend at low speed, just until the dry ingredients are moistened. Be careful not to overmix.

4. Let the dough sit for at least 1 hour to become evenly moistened. It may be covered and refrigerated overnight.

5. Heat the oven to 425°F. Lightly flour a 9-inch round cake or tart pan. Line a sheet pan with parchment paper.

6. Divide the dough into 2 equal pieces, and press 1 into the round pan, to shape it. Turn the dough disk out onto a lightly floured work surface, and cut it into 8 equal wedges. Repeat with the other half of the dough.

7. Arrange the wedges on the lined sheet pan, brush them lightly with the 4 tablespoons of cream, and sprinkle with the AA sugar.

8. Bake for 15 to 20 minutes, until golden brown. Cool on a rack. ✳

Continued on page 6

Variation: Drop Scones

If the wedge shape is just too structured for you, instead of letting the dough sit in step 4, simply drop it from a large wooden spoon onto the sheet pan immediately after mixing. Reduce the baking time to 12 minutes. The yield will be 24 small scones, unless you have a big spoon.

Variation: Cranberry Scones

Omit the dried fruit, and add 2 cups of fresh or frozen cranberries. Do not soak the fruit. Add 4 tablespoons of orange extract in step 2.

Variation: Blueberry Scones

Instead of the dried fruit use 2 cups of frozen blueberries and 1 teaspoon of lemon extract. (Frozen blueberries work very well; fresh ones tend to get mashed in the mixing.) Proceed as for Cranberry Scones.

Danish Dough

Greg Tompkins

This is the Tassajara Bread Bakery's recipe with instructions by Chef Bo Friberg. I apprenticed with Bo as a student at the California Culinary Academy and later had the great pleasure of returning to teach with him as a chef / instructor.

Because Danish dough takes time, it's a good idea to make a large batch (this recipes yields 6 to 7 pounds of dough). Then divide it into useful amounts, and freeze what you aren't going to use right away. The dough comes back beautifully when thawed under refrigeration. Be sure to thaw it until there are no parts still frozen in the interior, and then proof it until it is half again as large.

8 1/2 sticks soft butter

8 cups bread flour

1/2 tablespoon ground cardamom

2 cups ice water

4 eggs

1 tablespoon vanilla extract

1 tablespoon finely grated orange rind

2 ounces wet (cake, fresh, or compressed) yeast

1. On a work surface, form 8 of the sticks of butter into a square approximately 10 inches on a side and the thickness of a butter stick. Cover with plastic wrap, and set aside.

2. In the large bowl of a mixer fitted with a dough hook, combine the flour, cardamom, and the remaining 1/2 stick of butter, and stir lightly to blend. Set aside.

3. In a large bowl, combine the water, eggs, vanilla, and orange rind. Crumble the yeast into the bowl. Set aside.

4. With the mixer on low speed, slowly add the egg mixture to the flour mixture, until it is moistened. Switch to medium speed, and knead about 6 minutes, until the dough is soft and elastic.

5. Let the dough rest, covered, for 10 minutes. Then turn it onto a lightly floured work surface.

6. Roll the dough out to a square approximately 14 inches on a side. Place the butter block diagonally in the center, so that it looks like a diamond against the square dough. Seal the dough around the butter block by pulling all the exposed dough triangles into the center.

7. Roll the dough out into a rectangle approximately 8 by 12 inches. Fold the dough in thirds as you would a business letter. Turn the dough 90°, and roll it out a second time. Fold it in thirds again.

8. Cover the dough with plastic wrap, and let it rest for 45 minutes in the refrigerator.

Continued on page 8

9. Remove the dough from the refrigerator, and repeat steps 7 and 8.

10. Remove the dough from the refrigerator, and roll it out into a rectangle ½ inch thick. Cover the dough, and return it to the refrigerator for 30 minutes.

11. Remove the dough, and shape it into individual pastries, or divide into 1-pound portions, wrap, and freeze for later use. ∗

Danish Raisin Snails

Greg Tompkins

✳

Here is the classic version of this favorite Danish pastry.

Serves 18

1/2 cup sugar

1/2 cup cinnamon

2 pounds Danish Dough
(recipe on page 7)

3 cups raisins,
soaked in water until plump

1/3 cup Simple Syrup
(recipe on page 193)

1/2 cup Fondant
(recipe on page 194)

1. In a small bowl, mix the sugar with the cinnamon to make cinnamon sugar. Set aside.

2. Roll out the dough so that it is 1/8 inch thick, 14 inches wide, and as long as it will go.

3. Sprinkle the raisins evenly on top, and cover the dough with the cinnamon sugar. Gently press the raisins and sugar into the dough by rolling a rolling pin lengthwise (from one 14-inch edge to the other) over the dough.

4. Starting from a 14-inch edge, roll the dough up evenly, like a jelly roll, stretching the edges, if necessary.

5. With the seam side down, cut the roll into slices about 3/4 inch thick.

6. Line 3 cookie sheets with parchment paper, and place the slices, cut side up and slightly apart, on the sheets, tucking the outside end of the dough under each snail. Allow the snails to rise in a warm place for about 25 minutes (depending on the temperature of the area), until they are half again as large as they were.

7. Heat the oven to 400°F.

8. Bake the snails for 20 minutes, until they are golden brown.

9. Remove them from the oven, and brush them immediately with the simple syrup.

10. When they have cooled to room temperature, drizzle the fondant over them. ✳

Continued on page 10

9

Variation: Danish Cinnamon Rolls

Omit the raisins, simple syrup, and fondant. In step 3, sprinkle the dough with half of the cinnamon sugar, and press it in gently with the rolling pin, starting from a long edge. Cut 2 sticks (½ pound) of butter into ⅛-inch-thick slices, and place them on the dough about 2 inches apart. Then sprinkle on the remaining cinnamon sugar. In step 4, start rolling from a long edge.

Danish Bear Claws

California Culinary Academy

✳

This recipe is simple, and, by varying the filling (using different combinations of cake crumbs),
you can alter the flavor of the bear claws.

Serves 10

1 pound Danish Dough
(recipe on page 7)

3 cups Bear Claw Filling
(recipe on page 12)

2 eggs

1 tablespoon water

³/4 cup sliced almonds

¹/4 cup Simple Syrup
(recipe on page 193)

¹/2 cup Fondant
(recipe on page 194)

1. Roll the dough into a rectangle ¹/8 inch thick, 9 inches wide, and as long as it will go. Cut it in half lengthwise to make 2 strips 4¹/2 inches wide.

2. Place the filling in a pastry bag fitted with a number 4 tip, and pipe it across the top half of each strip.

3. Whisk the eggs with the water to make a wash, and brush the lower half of each dough strip with a fourth of the wash. Fold the lower half over the top half to encase the filling. Using the heel of your hand, lightly flatten the edges to seal the dough.

4. Using a paring knife, cut 1¹/2-inch incisions about ³/4 inch apart along the lightly flattened area of the dough, to make the "claws."

5. Brush the top of the dough with the remaining egg wash. Sprinkle the sliced almonds over the top.

6. Line a cookie sheet with parchment paper.

7. Cut the dough into pieces 4 to 5 inches wide. Shake any loose almonds off, and place the bear claws a little apart on the cookie sheet. Bend each uncut edge slightly into a semicircle, so that the "claws" separate a bit.

8. Cover the cookie sheet loosely, and place it in a warm area, until the bear claws are half again as big as they were.

9. Heat the oven to 425°F.

10. Bake the bear claws for 15 to 18 minutes, until they are golden brown.

11. Remove them from the oven, and brush them immediately with the simple syrup.

12. Cool them to room remperature, and ice them with the fondant.

Continued on page 12

Bear Claw Filling

¹/₂ pound (2 sticks) butter

2 cups sugar

1 pound almond paste

1 pound ground or chopped nuts
(or cake crumbs, or a combination)

About ¹/₂ cup Pastry Cream
(recipe on page 195)

1. In a medium mixer bowl, cream together the butter, sugar, and almond paste, a third at a time.

2. Stir in the nuts.

3. Add the pastry cream 2 tablespoons at a time, as needed to achieve a mixture that is pipable but still quite firm. (You may not need all the pastry cream.) (Yield: about 4 cups.) *

Marmalade Muffins with Streusel

Greg Tompkins

✳

When making these muffins it is important to imbed the marmalade in the center of the batter and seal it in
with the remaining batter. If the marmalade comes in contact with the muffin cup walls, the sugar in it
will caramelize and stick, and the muffins will be difficult to remove.

Serves 12

Streusel

2 tablespoons all-purpose flour

1/4 cup sugar

1/2 teaspoon cinnamon

2 tablespoons butter

Muffins

2 1/8 cups all-purpose flour

1/4 cup sugar

1 teaspoon baking powder

1/4 teaspoon baking soda

1/4 teaspoon salt

1/4 teaspoon ground ginger

1 egg, lightly beaten

1/4 cup salad oil

1 cup buttermilk

1/4 cup orange (or lemon) marmalade

Streusel

1. Combine the flour, sugar, and cinnamon in a small bowl. Cut
   in the butter to form a coarse meal. Refrigerate or freeze until
   needed.

Muffins

2. Combine the flour, half of the sugar, the baking powder, baking
   soda, salt, and ginger in a medium bowl, and stir to blend.
   Set aside.

3. Combine the egg, oil, buttermilk, and remaining sugar in a large
   bowl, and whisk vigorously to blend.

4. Beat the flour mixture into the egg mixture until just combined.
   Do not overmix (or the baked muffins will have tunnels in
   them).

5. Heat the oven to 375°F. Grease a 12-cup muffin pan, and brush
   the top surface of the pan lightly with a little salad oil.

6. Place a heaping tablespoon of batter in each muffin cup. Make a
   depression in the batter, and fill it with a teaspoon of marmalade.
   Cover the filling completely with the remaining batter, and top
   with the streusel.

7. Bake the muffins for 25 to 30 minutes, until golden brown.
   Cool the muffins in the pan for 5 minutes, then turn them out
   onto a rack. Serve warm. ✳

Giant Fruit Popover

Dan Bowe

✳

Not only does this dish taste good, but I think it also looks impressive on the buffet table.
It's not quite an omelet and not quite a soufflé either; it's in its own category.

Serves 4

Filling

2 6- to 7-ounce Granny Smith (or other firm) apples, peeled, cored, and sliced $1/4$ inch thick

4 tablespoons butter

$1/4$ cup granulated sugar

$1/8$ teaspoon ground cinnamon

Pinch ground coriander

$1/8$ teaspoon grated fresh ginger

4 ounces dried fruit, chopped (use a combination, such as pears, apricots, and cherries)

1 tablespoon fresh lemon juice

Batter

3 large eggs

$1^1/3$ cups milk, at room temperature

$1^1/2$ tablespoons melted butter

1 teaspoon vanilla extract

$1^1/3$ cups all-purpose flour

2 tablespoons brown sugar

$1/2$ teaspoon salt

2 tablespoons confectioners' sugar
(for garnish)

Filling

1. Heat the oven to 425°F.

2. In a medium skillet, sauté the apples in the butter over medium-high heat for 10 minutes.

3. Add the sugar, and sauté for 10 minutes more.

4. Add the cinnamon, coriander, and ginger. Cook over medium-high heat just until the apples soften and turn golden brown and the sugar starts to caramelize.

5. Stir in the dried fruit and lemon juice, remove from the heat, and let cool slightly.

6. Pour the apple mixture into the bottom of a pie pan (or quiche dish or ovenproof nonstick pan).

Batter

7. Combine all the batter ingredients in a food processor, and pulse for 40 seconds, until smooth, scraping down the sides. (Or, if you prefer, combine them by hand with a whisk or in a mixer.)

8. Pour the batter carefully and slowly over the apple mixture, and bake for 15 minutes at 425°F. Then reduce the heat to 350°F, and bake 20 minutes more. Do not open the oven door, or the popover, like a soufflé, may fall.

9. Remove from the oven, sprinkle with the confectioners' sugar, and cut into wedges. ✳

Roasted Vegetable Bread Pudding

Dan Bowe

This is a dish that my mother used to serve on especially cold days when I was growing up.
There were never problems getting my brothers and sisters to eat our vegetables on those days.

Serves 8

1 2-pound butternut (or Danish) squash, halved lengthwise and seeded

Salt and pepper to taste

3/4 teaspoon dried thyme

3/4 teaspoon dried rubbed sage

2 cloves garlic, crushed flat

1 small yellow onion
(5 to 6 ounces), halved lengthwise

2 teaspoons olive oil

1/2 cup diced fennel bulb,
cut into 1/2-inch pieces

1/2 medium green bell pepper,
cut into 1/2-inch dice

1 cup roasted (or light) vegetable (or chicken) stock
(recipe on page 185 or 186)

1/4 pound mushrooms, coarsely chopped

4 large eggs

3/4 cup cream (or half-and-half)

1/2 cup grated Monterey Jack cheese

1/2 cup crumbled blue cheese

1/2 cup coarsely chopped parsley

8 slices day-old (or toasted) hearty bread,
sliced 1/2 inch thick

1. Heat the oven to 400°F. Line a cookie sheet with aluminum foil.

2. Season the squash halves with some of the salt and pepper, 1/2 teaspoon of the thyme, and 1/2 teaspoon of the sage. Place 1 clove of the garlic into each squash cavity, and then place an onion half, cut side up, into each cavity, pressing it in, if necessary, so the top does not stick out.

3. Place the squash, cut side down, on the cookie sheet, making sure that the halves lie flat. Bake for 20 minutes.

4. Remove the cookie sheet, and lower the oven heat to 350°F.

5. Peel the squash, and dice the flesh into 1-inch cubes. (Yield: about 2 cups.)

6. Dice the onion, and mince the garlic.

7. Heat the oil in a large saucepan, and sauté the onion, fennel, and bell pepper for 5 minutes. Add the garlic, and sauté for 2 minutes more.

8. Add the stock, squash, mushrooms, remaining sage, and remaining thyme, and bring to a boil. Season with more salt and pepper, and let simmer, uncovered, for 10 minutes, until the stock is slightly reduced and has thickened. Remove from the heat.

9. In a medium bowl, combine the eggs, cream, cheeses, and parsley.

10. To assemble the bread pudding, butter a 2-quart casserole, and line the bottom with 2 to 3 slices of the bread, broken to fit and pressed in to form a fairly solid base. Pour a third of the squash mixture and a third of the egg mixture over the bread. Repeat with another third of each twice more, pressing the bread in gently, and ending with the egg mixture.

11. Bake for 45 minutes, or until set. ✳

Italian Frittata with Artichoke Hearts and Roasted Red Onions

Lars Kronmark

✳

This frittata reminds me of the Danish *eggekage* with freshly cut chives and thick, crisp, sweet bacon that my mother made all summer long, back on my parents' farm. We ate it hot or cold, and even the next day in my school lunch this frittata-style dish really tasted great with pumpernickel.

Serves 4

3 red onions, unpeeled,
cut in half lengthwise

2 tablespoons balsamic (or red wine) vinegar

8 cooked artichoke hearts,
cut in half lengthwise

1/2 teaspoon fresh oregano, chopped

Salt and freshly ground black pepper to taste

2 tablespoons light olive oil

10 eggs

1/4 cup water

1/2 cup Parmesan cheese

1. Heat the oven to 350°F.

2. Place the onions in a baking dish. Pour the vinegar over them, cover the dish, and roast for 45 minutes. Remove from the oven, and set aside.

3. Toss the artichoke hearts with the oregano and a pinch each of the salt and pepper in a medium bowl.

4. Remove the onion skins, and cut the onions into lengthwise strips 1/4 inch wide. Add to the artichokes, and toss. Add 1/2 tablespoon of the oil, and toss. Set aside.

5. In a medium bowl, whip the eggs with the water for 3 to 4 minutes. Add about a pinch each of the salt and pepper.

6. Heat the remaining 1 1/2 tablespoons of olive oil in a 9-inch, long-handled, overproof pan, and tilt to coat all sides. Add the egg mixture to the hot pan, turn the heat to its lowest setting, and cook for 2 to 3 minutes, to set the edges.

7. Transfer the pan to the oven, and bake, uncovered, for about 10 minutes.

8. Take the frittata out of the oven, and quickly add the artichoke mixture, spreading it to within 1 inch of the edges. Return the pan to the oven, and bake another 10 minutes.

9. Test by gently touching the center of the frittata. When there is no liquid in the center, it is done.

10. To serve, sprinkle the Parmesan cheese on top. ✳

Plain Omelet

Lars Kronmark

✳

I have never forgotten the omelet demonstration that chef-instructor Sorensen did when
I was in chef school in Copenhagen. There was not one wrinkle, not one brown spot. Try it.

Serves 1

3 eggs

1 tablespoon water (or milk)

Salt to taste

Freshly ground white pepper to taste

1 tablespoon clarified butter

Filling (see variations, below) (optional)

1. In a small bowl, beat the eggs with the water. Mix in the salt and pepper.

2. Heat the butter in a medium nonstick skillet. Use low heat for dessert omelets, because they should not be browned. Use higher heat for breakfast and lunch omelets.

3. Pour the egg mixture into the skillet, and stir with a firm rubber spatula, bringing the edges toward the middle to firm up the mixture on the bottom. Cook for 3 to 6 minutes, depending on how well done you like your eggs.

4. Tilt the skillet away from you, raising the handle 25° to 30°, and bang the handle with your fist to tap the omelet down away from you, forcing it to slide to the edge of the skillet. Keep it there while you carefully roll the egg that is still very soft out to the upper part of the pan. Then roll it back again. Repeat a couple of times, until the omelet is done to your liking.

5. Add filling, if you wish, in the middle of the omelet, and fold the egg over the filling. Turn the omelet upside down onto a plate. Place a kitchen towel over the omelet, and, using your hands over the towel, reshape the omelet to get a cross between a banana and a cigar. ✳

Variation: Omelet with Cheese

Heat the oven to 400°F. Use ¼ cup of grated soft cheese. Goat cheese, brie, and mozzarella are great. I like to use sharp cheddar and Monterey Jack together. Cut 1 slice of each into strips and set aside. Grate the rest, and add it to the omelet. After turning the omelet onto the plate in step 5, lay the strips of cheese on top in a zigzag pattern. Place the omelet in the hot oven for 1 minute. Serve.

Continued on page 20

Variation: Omelet with Fresh Fruit

Heat a broiler. Use about 2 ounces of the fruit of your choice. Strawberries, raspberries, and similar fruits are best. Cut large fruit into ½-inch pieces. Sprinkle the fruit with a few drops of lemon juice and sweet liqueur (if desired), and toss. Add the fruit to the middle of the omelet, and fold closed as described in step 5. Sprinkle 1 tablespoon of confectioners' sugar on top of the omelet. Place the omelet in the broiler for less than 1 minute, until the sugar browns and caramelizes. Or heat a metal skewer until very hot, and press it down on top of the omelet after sprinkling on the sugar. This makes the omelet look grilled.

Cranberry-Chestnut-Turkey Sausage Patties

Dan Bowe

✳

Your own sausage is so much healthier than fat-laden sausage from the store that there is really no excuse for not making it yourself. This recipe is especially wonderful during the holidays, as it combines a lot of the holiday flavors.

Serves 6

1 pound ground turkey

1/2 pound ground chicken

2 teaspoons minced dried cranberries

2 tablespoons canned chestnut puree

1 teaspoon ground allspice

1 teaspoon dried thyme

1 teaspoon dried rosemary, crushed or ground

1 teaspoon dried rubbed sage

4 teaspoons finely minced yellow onion

1 teaspoon minced garlic

1/2 teaspoon salt

1/2 teaspoon pepper

1. Combine all the ingredients, and mix well.

2. Form into 2½-inch patties, and cook over medium-high heat in a nonstick pan. ✳

Variation: Pork and Lamb Sausage Patties

Omit the turkey and chicken. Substitute 1 pound ground pork and 1/2 pound ground lamb.

Oven-Roasted Home Fries

Dan Bowe

✳

Here is a reduced-fat version of home fries, with great flavor, crispness, and color, achieved by roasting the potatoes
in a hot oven with a very small amount of oil. A layer of onions under the potatoes perfumes them with flavor,
while the potatoes insulate the onions from burning and turning bitter.

Serves 4

1 1/4 pounds small red (new) potatoes,
halved (or quartered)

2 teaspoons olive oil

3/4 teaspoon salt

1/4 teaspoon black pepper

1/4 teaspoon garlic powder

3/4 cup sliced yellow onions
in 1/4- to 1/2-inch strips

1. Heat the oven to 425°F. Line a sheet pan with parchment paper.

2. In a large bowl, toss the potatoes with the oil, salt, pepper, and
garlic powder.

3. Arrange the onions in a single layer, very close together, on the
sheet pan.

4. Spread the potato mixture on top of the onions, also in a single
layer.

5. Roast for 20 to 25 minutes, until the potatoes are browned on
the outside and soft inside. ✳

Starters

Crostini with Herbed Goat Cheese and Marinated Sun-Dried Tomatoes

Johnathan Robinette

✳

This easy and quick taste treat is ideal for spur-of-the-moment entertaining. A favorite item on restaurant menus, *crostini* will delight your guests with only minimal effort on your part.

Serves 4

Crostini

1 baguette

¾ cup virgin olive oil

3 cloves garlic, halved

Goat Cheese Spread

¾ cup (6 ounces) sun-dried tomatoes

2 tablespoons balsamic vinegar

3 tablespoons extra virgin olive oil

½ cup (4 ounces) goat cheese, softened

1 tablespoon chopped fresh herbs (oregano, thyme, and/or basil)

Salt to taste

16 fresh basil leaves

Crostini

1. Heat the oven to 200°F.

2. Cut the baguette diagonally into rounds ¼ inch thick. (Yield: about 30.)

3. Heat a little of the olive oil in a small sauté pan over moderate heat. When it is hot, fry the baguette rounds, a few at a time, until brown and crisp. Remove the rounds, and place them on paper towels to drain the excess oil.

4. Rub each side of the rounds with the garlic. Keep the *crostini* warm in the oven until ready to spread. You may store extra *crostini* in an airtight plastic container at room temperature.

Goat Cheese Spread

5. Soak the tomatoes in a small bowl of warm water until softened, about 5 minutes. Drain them, squeeze out the excess moisture, coarsely chop the tomatoes, and place them in a clean bowl.

6. Add the vinegar and oil to the tomatoes, cover, and refrigerate.

7. Place the cheese in a food processor, and process until smooth, about 15 seconds. Mix in the herbs and salt.

8. Spread 1 teaspoon of the cheese mixture on each of 16 warm *crostini*. Place 1 basil leaf in the center of the cheese, and spoon ½ tablespoon of the tomato mixture next to the basil. Serve at room temperature, or refrigerate for later use. ✳

Continued on page 26

Variation:
Crostini with Kalamata Olive Tapenade

3/4 cup (6 ounces) Kalamata
(or black) olives, pits removed

4 cloves garlic

1/4 cup Italian parsley leaves, loosely packed

Jalapeño pepper to taste, seeded

1/2 cup extra virgin olive oil

16 *Crostini* (recipe on page 24)

16 anchovy fillets, drained of oil and
rolled into rounds

This flexible tapenade can be made with either imported or domestic black olives. For a different taste sensation, substitute green olives. Use the tapenade to top *crostini* or as a condiment to accompany chicken, fish, or vegetable dishes.

1. Place the olives, garlic, parsley, and pepper in a food processor, and process for 3 to 5 seconds, until coarsely chopped.

2. With the processor running, slowly pour the oil through the feed tube, and incorporate it into the olive mixture.

3. Spread the mixture on the *crostini,* and garnish each with a rolled anchovy fillet. ✳

Bruschetta with Mushrooms and Smoked Provolone

Linda Carucci

Redolent of garlic and fresh herbs, these savory toasts make a great hors d'oeuvre or buffet side dish.

Serves 4

Bruschetta

1 loaf crusty Italian bread, ends removed, sliced diagonally into 8 ³⁄₄-inch-thick slices

⅓ cup olive oil

1 clove garlic, halved crosswise

⅔ cup grated Asiago (or Romano) cheese

3 tablespoons chopped fresh rosemary, sage, and/or oregano

Topping

1 tablespoon olive oil

1 pound mushrooms, sliced ¼ inch thick

3 cloves garlic, minced

1 tablespoon chopped fresh thyme

¼ cup dry white (or red) wine

½ teaspoon salt

¼ teaspoon freshly ground black pepper

1 pinch crushed red chili flakes

6 ounces smoked provolone, cut into ½-inch cubes

⅓ cup diced roasted red pepper (fresh or bottled with brine rinsed off)

4 to 6 leaves fresh basil, chopped

Bruschetta

1. Heat a broiler.

2. Place the slices of bread on a baking sheet. Brush the tops with the oil, and rub them with the cut sides of the garlic.

3. Sprinkle the cheese evenly over the bread, and top with a sprinkling of the herbs.

4. Broil for 2 to 3 minutes, until the cheese melts.

5. Remove the baking sheet, and set aside. Leave the broiler on.

Topping

6. Heat the oil in a nonstick skillet over high heat. Add the mushrooms, and sauté until they begin to give up their juices. Add the garlic and thyme, and sauté until the garlic just begins to brown. Add the wine, and continue to sauté for 6 to 8 minutes, until there is no more liquid in the pan. Season with the salt, pepper, and chili flakes.

7. Distribute the mushroom mixture on top of the *bruschetta*. Top with the smoked provolone cubes, and return the baking sheet to the broiler. Broil until the cheese just begins to melt. (Watch carefully, and turn the pan if necessary.) Remove the baking sheet from the broiler.

8. Mix the red pepper with the basil, and garnish each *bruschetta* with a little of the mixture. Serve immediately. *

Brie and Arugula Open-Faced Sandwiches

Johnathan Robinette

✳

Prepared with thin slices of sourdough baguette, these open-faced sandwiches make a simple and colorful hors d'oeuvre.

Serves 4

1 red bell pepper

4 slices fresh sourdough bread, sliced diagonally

1 clove garlic, halved crosswise

6 ounces double-cream (or triple-cream) brie, cut into 4 pieces

1 cup fresh arugula leaves

1. Heat a broiler.

2. Spear the pepper with a long, wood-handled fork, and roast it over an open flame until the skin is blistered (or char the pepper under a broiler, turning to char all sides evenly).

3. Enclose the pepper in a self-seal plastic bag for 10 minutes, to loosen the skin.

4. Meanwhile, toast the sourdough slices lightly. Rub them with the cut sides of the garlic.

5. Remove the pepper skin, and seed and dice the pepper.

6. Top the sourdough slices with the brie, and broil them until the cheese is slightly melted.

7. Remove the slices from the broiler, and top with the arugula and diced pepper. ✳

Afternoon Tea Sandwiches

Teresa Douglas/Mitchell

Typical tea fare, these sandwiches make small, elegant bites. After all, afternoon tea originated as a snack
once the concept of luncheon was introduced and supper became a late evening affair.

Tea sandwiches are among the easiest foods to dress up with cut shapes and a variety of pretty garnishes.

Serves 20

Smoked Salmon and Goat Cheese Mousse

4 ounces goat cheese

4 ounces cream cheese

1 tablespoon dry white wine

3 tablespoons chopped chives

2 ounces smoked salmon slices

Victorian Creamed Butter and Cucumber

1 cup unsalted butter

1 tablespoon heavy cream

1/4 teaspoon Dijon mustard

1 teaspoon lemon juice

Salt and pepper to taste

1 thinly sliced English cucumber

Smoked Chicken and Dill

1 cup smoked chicken

4 ounces cream cheese

1/4 cup sour cream

3 tablespoons minced fresh dill

Salt and pepper to taste

20 slices bread, various kinds, thinly sliced

3 teaspoons capers

3 teaspoons grated lemon zest

3 teaspoons fresh dill weed

3 teaspoons chopped fresh chives

1. Combine all the ingredients for the smoked salmon mousse in a food processor, and process until smooth. Place in a pastry bag.

2. Combine all the ingredients except the cucumber for the Victorian creamed butter in a food processor, and process until smooth. Place in a pastry bag.

3. Combine all the ingredients for the smoked chicken and dill in a food processor, and process until smooth. Place in a pastry bag.

4. Cut each slice of bread into 4 triangles or 3 diamonds.

5. Pipe a spread onto each piece of bread. Place 1 to 2 slices of English cucumber on each Victorian creamed butter sandwich.

6. Garnish the salmon sandwiches with a sprinkling of about 1/4 teaspoon of capers or lemon zest, the cucumber with the chives, and the chicken with the dill. *

Pesto Tarts with Glazed Leeks and Smoked Salmon

Tamara Frey

This is a great dish for a party, because guests can assemble their own tarts. Present a tray of tart shells and bowls of pesto, glazed leeks, grated Romano cheese, tomato, and smoked salmon.

Golden tomatoes are beautiful in this pesto. Unlike classic pesto, which uses basil and a good deal of oil, this recipe uses tomato and less oil, so the color is different. The pesto is also wonderful on a smoked salmon pizza.

Serves 6

Tarts

1 1/2 teaspoons active dry yeast

1 1/2 teaspoons sweetener (honey, maple syrup, or sucanat—an organic cane sugar)

1/4 cup warm water

2/3 cup cool water

2 tablespoons olive oil

1 cup whole-wheat flour

1 3/4 cups white flour

1 teaspoon salt

4 tablespoons mixed fresh herbs (parsley, chives, cilantro, basil, rosemary, sage, etc.) in equal parts

Glazed Leeks

1 large leek, julienned

1 teaspoon olive oil

2 tablespoons white wine

Tarts

1. Dissolve the yeast and sweetener in the warm water in a medium bowl. Let sit for about 10 minutes, until foamy. Then add the cool water and oil.

2. Heat the oven to 350°F. Lightly oil a baking sheet.

3. Place the flours, salt, and herbs in the bowl of a food processor. With the motor running, slowly pour in the yeast mixture until the dough comes away from the sides of the bowl. Add more flour if needed, to form a soft dough.

4. Roll the dough out 1/4 inch thick. Using a 4-inch biscuit cutter, cut out the tarts. (Yield: about 12 tarts.) Crimp the edges between your floured thumb and forefinger, as you would crimp a piecrust, to form a decorative raised edge. Place the tart shells on the baking sheet, and prick the shells a few times with a fork.

5. Bake for 6 to 8 minutes, until the bottoms of the tart shells are golden.

Glazed Leeks

6. In a small sauté pan, sauté the leeks in the oil for 5 to 6 minutes. Deglaze the pan with the wine. Cover, and simmer about 5 minutes more. Remove to a serving bowl.

Continued on page 32

Pesto

1 medium tomato

2 cups mixed fresh basil, parsley, and cilantro in equal parts

4 large cloves garlic

4 tablespoons freshly grated Romano cheese

2 tablespoons toasted pine nuts (or almonds, walnuts, or sunflower seeds)

3 tablespoons extra virgin olive oil

1 tablespoon lime juice (or lemon juice)

Garnish

1 large tomato, chopped

3 tablespoons grated Romano cheese

4 tablespoons julienned smoked salmon

Pesto

7. Core the tomato, and simmer it in water for about 5 seconds. Drain, and slip the skin off. Cut the tomato in half crosswise. Squeeze out the seeds. Place the pulp in a food processor.

8. Add all of the other pesto ingredients, and process for 10 seconds, until pureed. Add more tomato or oil if necessary to form a thick sauce.

9. To serve, spread pesto on a tart shell, and top with leeks, chopped tomato, Romano, and salmon. *

Gravlax on Rye Bread with Mustard-Dill Sauce

Lars Kronmark

This open-faced sandwich is thoroughly Scandinavian. As I tell my students, the Vikings loved salmon. Gravlax started when more salmon was caught than could be eaten fresh. The rest was wrapped in burlap with salt and wild dill and buried in the frozen tundra.

Tak for mad ("enjoy" in Danish).

Serves 25

Gravlax

1/2 salmon fillet with skin on (about 5 pounds)

1/2 cup salt

1 cup sugar

1 tablespoon ground fennel

1 cup fresh (or 1/2 cup dried) dill weed, chopped

Mustard-Dill Sauce

1/2 cup mild Dijon mustard

2 tablespoons lemon juice

3/4 cup brown sugar, loose (not packed)

1 tablespoon chopped fresh
(or 1/2 tablespoon dried) dill weed

Salt and pepper to taste

25 slices rye bread, 1/4 inch thick

4 tablespoons plus 1/2 teaspoon butter

25 to 50 leaves butter lettuce
(1 to 2 leaves per slice of bread)

50 large sprigs fresh dill

Gravlax

1. Lay the salmon, skin side down, in a 2-inch-deep dish, and sprinkle the salt, sugar, fennel, and dill on top, in that order, packing them down around and on top of the salmon with your hand.

2. Cover the salmon with plastic wrap. Place 2 plates upside down on top of the salmon, and place a weight (such as a 16-ounce can of fruit) on top of each plate.

3. Place the dish in the refrigerator for 3 days. Once a day, take the dish out, unwrap it, and pour off the excess liquid.

4. After 3 days, remove the coated salmon to a cutting board, and slice it very thinly into 75 slices. Set aside.

Mustard-Dill Sauce

5. Place all the sauce ingredients in the top of a double boiler, and cook for 6 minutes, stirring occasionally, until the sugar and salt have dissolved. Remove from the heat, and chill.

6. When the sauce is chilled, mix it well with a whisk.

7. To serve, spread each slice of the bread evenly with 1/2 teaspoon of the butter. Place 1 to 2 leaves of the butter lettuce on the slice. Lay 3 slices of gravlax on top, covering the slice of bread. Spoon 2 to 3 teaspoons of the sauce on top, and garnish with 2 sprigs of dill. *

Spinach and Corn Strudel

Lars Kronmark

✳

Making dough is a chapter by itself, so what could be greater than flaky and tasty prepared phyllo dough.
I even use it for tarts and pies. Where was this item when I started cooking? Have fun with this dish.

Serves 4

1 cup part-skim ricotta cheese

2 tablespoons Parmesan cheese

1¹/₂ cups fresh (or frozen) corn kernels

2 egg whites

¹/₂ teaspoon grated lemon zest

Freshly grated nutmeg to taste

Salt to taste

Black pepper to taste

1 tablespoon olive oil

5 cups packed raw spinach

4 sheets phyllo dough

4 tablespoons melted butter

1¹/₂ cups Fresh Tomato Sauce
(recipe on page 181)

1. Heat the oven to 400°F. Lightly flour a sheet pan.

2. In a medium bowl, mix the ricotta, Parmesan, corn, egg whites, lemon zest, nutmeg, salt, and pepper until well combined. Set aside.

3. Heat the oil in a large skillet, and sauté the spinach over medium heat, sitrring, for 3 to 5 minutes, until soft. Dry the spinach by wrapping it in a cloth towel and squeezing it gently. Chill it in the refrigerator for 10 minutes.

4. Brush a sheet of the phyllo with 1 tablespoon of the butter. Place a second sheet on top of the first and brush it with another tablespoon of butter. Repeat with the other sheets to make a stack.

5. With the long side of the phyllo toward you, spoon the ricotta mixture onto the bottom third of the dough, and spread the spinach on top of it.

6. Roll the phyllo up from the bottom, like a log, tucking the sides in, so the filling won't fall out. Place the roll on the sheet pan, and bake for 20 minutes, until golden.

7. To serve, ladle the tomato sauce onto 4 plates. Cut 4 slightly diagonal 1-inch crosswise slices of strudel, and place each one, a bit off center and cut side up, on a plate, so that the pinwheel design of the filling shows. Slice the remaining strudel into 4 pieces, each with a straight crosswise edge and a slightly diagonal edge. Stand each slice on its straight edge, like a small tower beside the strudel on a plate. ✳

Apple-Potato Galettes with Goat Cheese

Michael Kalanty

This versatile dish may be served as an appetizer or a cheese and salad course; omit the field greens,
and you have a crisp accompaniment to grilled veal chops or poultry.

Serves 4

2 tablespoons clarified butter

2 large baking potatoes, peeled and
thinly sliced (do not soak in water)

About 1/2 teaspoon salt

1 large baking apple (Granny Smith,
Stayman Winesap, etc.), peeled, halved,
and thinly sliced (do not soak in water)

6 ounces goat cheese

2 teaspoons finely chopped fresh chives

2 teaspoons finely chopped fresh parsley

1/3 teaspoon freshly cracked black pepper

3 tablespoons heavy cream

2 slices lightly toasted bread,
(preferably French),
ground into crumbs (1/4 cup)

1/2 pound *mesclun*
(or mixed salad greens)

1 ounce extra virgin olive oil

1 tablespoon red wine vinegar
(or apple cider vinegar)

1. Melt 1½ tablespoons of the clarified butter in a large, nonstick sauté pan over medium-high heat.

2. Using half of the potato slices, overlap them to form 4 5-inch rounds in the pan. Sprinkle with 1/8 teaspoon of the salt. Divide the apple slices among the rounds, overlapping them to form a second layer. Sprinkle with another 1/8 teaspoon of salt. Top with overlapped slices of the remaining potatoes. Sprinkle with 1/8 teaspoon salt. Press down on the galettes with a spatula to even them. Reduce the heat to medium-low.

3. Cover the pan, and cook for 10 to 12 minutes, until the bottoms of the galettes are golden and crusty. As the edges brown, shake the pan or slide a metal spatula under the galettes to loosen them.

4. Remove the galettes, and add the remaining ½ tablespoon of clarified butter to the pan. Invert the galettes onto a small plate, and carefully slide them back into the pan.

5. Cook, uncovered, for 7 to 10 minutes more, until the galettes are well browned. Remove them to drain on paper towels.

6. While the galettes are cooking, beat the goat cheese with the chives, parsley, a pinch of the salt, and the pepper. Then beat in the cream.

7. Divide the cheese mixture into 4 parts, and form them into cakes about 2 inches in diameter. Coat the cakes with the bread crumbs, and place them on a plate lined with parchment paper. Refrigerate for 30 minutes.

8. Adjust the oven rack to the middle of the oven. Heat the oven to 425°F. Line a baking tray with parchment paper.

Continued on page 38

9. Place the galettes on the baking tray, and top each galette with a chilled goat cheese cake.

10. Place in the oven, and bake for 7 to 8 minutes, until the bread crumbs are golden and the galettes are heated through.

11. While the galettes are baking, combine the *mesclun* with the oil, vinegar, and remaining salt in a large bowl. Toss to mix. Divide the greens among 4 serving plates.

12. Place a galette beside the greens on each plate. ✳

Grilled Seasonal Vegetables with Aioli

Lars Kronmark

✳

The first time I tasted grilled sliced vegetables, I was at a Napa Valley winery where the chef
grilled local vegetables over hot mesquite. What a treat! Just thinking about it brings back the flavor of
my introduction to this super tasty and very seasonal dish as if it was yesterday.

Serves 4

Aioli

2 egg yolks

3 cloves garlic, minced

¼ teaspoon salt

⅛ teaspoon cayenne

2 teaspoons lemon juice

3 tablespoons finely diced fresh herbs
(such as rosemary or basil) (optional)

1 cup olive oil

Grilled Vegetables

4 firm zucchini, any color, sliced

2 red bell peppers, halved and seeded

1 eggplant (or 2 small Japanese eggplants), sliced

8 shiitake mushrooms (or large white mushrooms),
stems removed

1 pound asparagus, bottom ⅓ trimmed

½ cup olive oil

¼ cup balsamic vinegar

4 cloves garlic, minced

½ teaspoon dried red pepper flakes

1 teaspoon dried oregano

Salt and freshly ground black pepper to taste

Aioli

1. In a 2-quart bowl, whisk together all the aioli ingredients except
   the oil for 1 minute.

2. While whisking, slowly add the oil in a steady stream for 3 to 4
   minutes. The aioli will have the consistency of mayonnaise.

3. Place in a small ceramic dish in the center of a large serving
   platter. Set aside.

Grilled Vegetables

4. Heat a grill until it is very hot.

5. Dry the zucchini, bell peppers, eggplant, mushrooms, and
   asparagus thoroughly.

6. Mix the oil, vinegar, garlic, pepper flakes, and oregano in a large
   bowl. Toss the vegetables in the bowl, and let them marinate
   for about 5 minutes, mixing periodically.

7. With tongs, lift out the vegetables, shake off excess marinade,
   and grill the vegetables for 6 to 8 minutes, until lightly colored
   on both sides.

8. Season with the salt and black pepper. Place around the aioli
   dip on the serving platter ✳

good

Wild Rice and Potato Pancakes
with Field Greens in Mustard Vinaigrette

Linda Carucci

The combination of wild rice with grated russet potato and yam creates a colorful pancake with unique textures.
If possible, serve these savory pancakes hot off the griddle.

Serves 4

3/4 cup peeled, grated russet potato

1/2 cup peeled, grated yam

1 cup cooked wild rice

1/4 cup diced onion

1 shallot, minced

1 tablespoon minced fresh thyme

1 teaspoon salt

1/4 teaspoon freshly ground pepper

2 eggs, lightly beaten

1/3 to 1/2 cup flour

2 tablespoons olive oil

8 cups field greens (mixed baby salad greens)

1 recipe Mustard Vinaigrette (recipe on page 42)

4 tablespoons Crème Fraîche (recipe on page 196)
(or sour cream) for garnish

1. Rinse the grated potato and yam in cold water, wrap in a towel, and squeeze dry.

2. In a medium bowl, mix the potato, yam, wild rice, onion, shallot, thyme, salt, and pepper together.

3. Stir in the eggs.

4. Fold in 1/3 cup of the flour, adding more if necessary to bind the batter.

5. Heat a skillet over medium heat, and add the olive oil. When the oil is warm, drop in a scant 1/4 cup of the batter for each pancake, and fry for about 2 minutes per side, until the pancakes are brown.

6. Toss the field greens with the mustard vinaigrette, and divide among 4 plates.

7. Arrange 2 or 3 pancakes on top of each plate of greens, and garnish with 1 tablespoon of the crème fraîche. Serve immediately. ✳

Continued on page 42

Mustard Vinaigrette

2 teaspoons minced shallot

1 teaspoon Dijon mustard

1 teaspoon whole-grain mustard

2 tablespoons balsamic vinegar

½ teaspoon salt

Pinch sugar

⅓ cup olive oil

Freshly ground black pepper (optional)

1. Place the shallot, mustards, vinegar, salt, and sugar in a small bowl, and whisk together.

2. While whisking, slowly drizzle in the olive oil. Whisk until the dressing is emulsified. Taste. If the dressing is too sharp, add another pinch of sugar. Add a bit of pepper if desired. (Yield: ½ cup.) *

Tabbouleh in Grape Leaves

Johnathan Robinette

✳

Tabbouleh has its roots in the Middle East. Made from bulgur, an ancient grain, tabbouleh is served cold, providing a nutritious, high-fiber dish. It can stand alone as an alternative to rice pilaf or be wrapped in grape leaves (or cucumber strips or endive leaves) for bite-size hors d'oeuvres.

Serves 10

1¼ cups (½ pound) fine bulgur

1 quart warm water

⅔ cup finely chopped onion

¾ cup finely chopped parsley

¼ cup coarsely chopped mint leaves

Juice of 2 lemons

1½ teaspoons salt

½ teaspoon pepper

½ cup finely diced tomato

½ cup peeled, seeded, and finely diced cucumber

½ cup extra virgin olive oil

10 pickled grape leaves

1. Soak the bulgur in the water for ½ hour. Drain in a fine-mesh colander, and press out the remaining water.

2. Place the bulgur in a mixing bowl. Add the onion, parsley, mint, and lemon juice. Mix.

3. Add the salt and pepper. Mix.

4. Stir in the tomato and cucumber. Slowly add the olive oil, and mix. Cover and refrigerate until you are ready to stuff the grape leaves.

5. Roll each grape leaf around 2 tablespoons of tabbouleh, and tuck the leaf ends in. Arrange the grape leaves around the edge of a serving platter with a mound of tabbouleh in the center. Refrigerate until serving time. ✳

Smoked Swordfish Carpaccio

Louie Jocson

A crisp chardonnay makes a wonderful combination with the smoky flavor of the swordfish.

Serves 6

6 ounces Smoked Swordfish (recipe below, or purchased), sliced paper thin

4 tablespoons olive oil

3 teaspoons lemon juice

2 tablespoons sliced leek

2 tablespoons diced tomato

2 tablespoons chopped fresh parsley

2 tablespoons capers

6 *Grissini* (recipe on page 110) (bread sticks)

2 cups baby arugula

2 tablespoons shaved Parmesan cheese

Freshly ground black pepper to taste

1. Fan the swordfish slices on the bottom of a large serving platter.

2. Drizzle 2 tablespoons of the olive oil and 1 teaspoon of the lemon juice over the fish.

3. Sprinkle the leek, tomato, parsley, and capers randomly on top.

4. Lay the *grissini,* parallel and slightly apart, across the center of the platter.

5. Toss the arugula with the remaining olive oil and lemon juice. Place it in the center of the platter, on top of the bread sticks (or at the side, if you prefer).

6. Top with the Parmesan and pepper. ✳

Smoked Swordfish

3 quarts plus 3 tablespoons water

1 cup salt

1 cup brown sugar

1 cup brandy

1 2-pound piece swordfish (small eye of round with skin on)

1 bay leaf

3 sprigs thyme

3 sprigs rosemary

1 tablespoon black peppercorns

1. Combine the 3 quarts of water, salt, brown sugar, and brandy in a medium pot.

2. Heat until the salt and sugar are dissolved in the liquid.

3. Remove from the heat, and let cool.

4. When the brine is cool, place the swordfish in it. Cover, refrigerate, and marinate for at least 15 hours.

5. Line a wok with aluminum foil, leaving 2 inches of excess foil overhanging the top of the wok.

Continued on page 46

6. Place ½ pound of hickory wood chips in the wok with the bay leaf, thyme, rosemary, and peppercorns, and moisten the mixture with the remaining 3 tablespoons of water.

7. Place a grill grate above the wood and herbs in the wok.

8. Remove the swordfish from the brine, and place it on the grill grate, resting on a skin side.

9. Cover the wok, and crimp the excess foil over the wok and lid to seal it so that the smoke will not escape. Place the wok over medium-low heat for 30 minutes. Then turn off the heat, and allow the fish to smoke for 1½ to 2 hours.

10. Remove the swordfish. When it is cool enough, wrap it in plastic, and refrigerate it until ready to use. It will keep for up to 3 days. (Yield: 1 pound, 10 ounces trimmed smoked swordfish.) *

Tomato and Red Onion Salad with Goat Cheese

Louie Jocson

This simple salad is so elegant and takes so little time to prepare, you'll quickly add it to your culinary repertoire.

Serves 4

5 tomatoes, peeled and quartered

1 red onion, sliced

6 to 7 large basil leaves,
cut into chiffonade

1 teaspoon garlic, minced

Pinch of salt

Cracked black pepper to taste

4 tablespoons balsamic vinegar

2 tablespoons extra virgin olive oil

4 ounces goat cheese, crumbled

English cucumber, sliced

1. Place the tomatoes and onion in a medium mixing bowl.

2. Add the basil and garlic, and mix gently.

3. Season with the salt and pepper.

4. Add the vinegar and oil, and toss.

5. Add the goat cheese, and toss lightly.

6. Garnish with slices of English cucumber. ✳

Antipasto Platter

Linda Carucci

✵

Add your favorite hot or cold seasonal hors d'oeuvres to create an original platter of texture and taste contrasts. Traditionally served before the meal in Italy, an antipasto platter makes a colorful addition to a festive buffet.

Serves 4

3 roasted garlic bulbs
(recipe on page 57, step 4)

6 each variety salt-cured black olives,
marinated green olives,
and brine-cured black olives

4 wedges (12 ounces) provolone
(or smoked provolone)

4 slices (1 ounce) Fresh Mozzarella
(recipe on page 50 or purchased)

4 thin slices ($^1/_2$ ounce) each coppa colla,
Italian salami, prosciutto, and / or mortadella

3 each color (red, yellow, and green)
grilled peppers (or marinated roasted peppers,
recipe on page 52, steps 1–5)

2 sprigs fresh basil

1 loaf (1 pound) crusty Italian bread, sliced

12 bread sticks

1. Place the roasted garlic bulbs in the center of a large platter. Arrange the olives, cheeses, cold cuts, and grilled peppers in separate sections on the platter, placing ingredients with contrasting colors beside each other.

2. Garnish with the basil.

3. Arrange the crusty bread and bread sticks next to the platter. ✵

Continued on page 50

Fresh Mozzarella

2 gallons water

1 pound plus ½ cup kosher salt

5 pounds mozzarella curd
(available from a commercial
cheese manufacturer)

1. Bring 1 gallon of the water to a boil. Reduce to a simmer, add the 1 pound of salt, and stir until the salt is completely dissolved. Pour this saline solution into a bowl or tub, and refrigerate until it is completely chilled.

2. Bring the remaining gallon of water to a boil, and add the remaining ½ cup of salt. Stir until the salt is dissolved. Keep the water very hot.

3. Using a chef's knife, shave all of the mozzarella curd into ¼-inch-thick slices in a large stainless steel bowl.

4. Pour a third of the hot salt water over the curd. Working quickly, mix the water and curd together with a wooden spatula, folding the curd over itself. When the water begins to resemble skim milk, pour it off.

5. Repeat step 4 with another third of the hot water. Then pour in the last third of hot water, and repeat the curd folding. Soon the curd should melt together into one mass, resembling a ball of melted cheese.

6. Place the bowl of cold saline solution on a work surface. Wearing rubber gloves, lift the mozzarella curd out of the hot water, and squeeze it between your thumb and index finger into balls, ranging in size anywhere from a golf ball to a baseball.

7. Place the balls in the cold saline solution, and let them float for 3 minutes. Turn them over in the solution, and let them float for another 3 minutes.

8. Store the mozzarella in a bowl of cold water (salted or unsalted, as you prefer). For best enjoyment, slice and serve within 2 hours. To store longer, refrigerate. (Yield: 5 pounds.) ✳

Baby Pumpkin Salad

Johnathan Robinette

✳

In the fall, markets are usually filled with baby pumpkins, which most people use only for decoration. These pumpkins are delicious; they have a sweet flavor similar to that of acorn squash. Here is an interesting recipe that uses both their flavor and their decorative qualities.

Serves 4

4 baby pumpkins

12 tablespoons Smoked Bacon Vinaigrette (recipe below)

4 cups loose seasonal baby greens (3 to 4 heads)

1/2 cup enoki mushrooms

8 baby corn cobs

16 chives

4 teaspoons toasted pumpkin seeds for garnish

1. Blanch the pumpkins in salted water for about 5 minutes, until soft and tender. Cut out the stems of the pumpkins and remove the seeds and stringy pulp.

2. Spoon 2 tablespoons of the vinaigrette into each pumpkin.

3. Arrange the greens, enoki mushrooms, corn, and chives in the pumpkins.

4. Place a filled pumpkin on each plate, and spoon the remaining vinaigrette evenly over the salads.

5. Sprinkle the toasted pumpkin seeds on top, and serve. To eat, cut the pumpkin open, and scoop out the flesh with the filling ingredients. ✳

Smoked Bacon Vinaigrette

1/4 cup lean, minced smoked bacon

1 1/2 teaspoons finely chopped garlic

2 tablespoons finely chopped onion

3 tablespoons brown sugar

2 tablespoons Dijon mustard

1/2 tablespoon coarsely ground black pepper

1/4 cup cider vinegar

1/2 cup olive oil

1. Place the bacon in a hot sauté pan, and cook until brown.

2. Drain off the fat.

3. Add the garlic and onion, and sauté until caramelized (brown).

4. Add the sugar, mustard, and black pepper. Cook over low heat for 1 minute.

5. Add the vinegar to the pan, and deglaze it. Pour the contents into a mixing bowl.

6. Slowly add the oil, mixing continuously to emulsify it. (Yield: 1 cup.) ✳

Marinated Five-Pepper Salad with Buffalo Mozzarella

Johnathan Robinette

Roasted peppers are simple to prepare and delicious. This salad takes advantage of the intense flavors created by roasting the peppers. If you buy small balls of buffalo mozzarella, cut them in quarters, leave the peppers in halves, and serve a quarter of cheese inside each half pepper.

Serves 6

3 red, 3 green, 3 yellow, and 3 orange bell peppers

4 tablespoons virgin olive oil

1 tablespoon finely chopped fresh basil

1 teaspoon finely chopped fresh oregano

1 teaspoon finely chopped fresh marjoram

1 teaspoon minced garlic

1 teaspoon minced shallot

2 tablespoons fresh lemon juice

1/4 teaspoon salt

1/2 teaspoon freshly cracked black pepper

1 tablespoon canola oil

1/4 cup sherry vinegar

1 pound buffalo mozzarella, (or fresh whole-milk mozzarella—recipe on page 50 or purchased)

Fresh opal basil leaves

1. Brush the peppers with 1 tablespoon of the olive oil.

2. Roast them over an open flame until the skin blackens and the peppers are tender all over.

3. Enclose the peppers in brown paper bags, and let them steam for about 10 minutes. Remove the blackened skin. Stem and seed the peppers, cut them into 1-inch wide strips, and place them in a ceramic dish.

4. In a small bowl, combine the chopped basil, oregano, marjoram, garlic, shallot, lemon juice, salt, and 1/4 teaspoon of the black pepper. Add the canola oil and 1 tablespoon of the remaining olive oil, and whisk to blend.

5. Pour the mixture over the peppers, cover, and refrigerate for 2 to 3 days.

6. To serve, drain the peppers, reserving the marinade. Arrange the peppers on a platter, alternating colors. Brush them lightly with the reserved marinade and the sherry vinegar.

7. Drain the mozzarella, pat it dry, and cut it into thin slices (or quarter the balls, if they are 3 inches in diameter or less). Place the mozzarella in the center of the platter, and brush with the remaining 2 tablespoons of olive oil. Sprinkle with the remaining black pepper, and garnish with the opal basil leaves. ✳

Curried Pumpkin Soup with Chutney Cream

Tamara Frey

✳

The presentation of this dish is like a van Gogh—a decorative vegetarian soup, served in a pumpkin shell.

Pumpkin seeds are highly nutritious and tasty. Toss them in a mixture of oil, soy sauce, and lime juice, spread them on a baking sheet, and bake them at 350°F for 15 minutes, stirring frequently, until they are toasted.

Serves 6

Chutney Cream

2 cups nonfat yogurt

1 Granny Smith apple

1 red onion, finely chopped

1 tablespoon minced fresh ginger

1/4 cup cider vinegar

1/4 cup sweetener (sugar, honey, or maple syrup)

1/4 teaspoon hot chili paste (or tabasco) (optional)

Pumpkin Soup

6 small (or 1 large) pie pumpkins (or winter squash) (enough to yield 4 cups pumpkin flesh while leaving a firm shell)

1 tablespoon olive oil (or butter)

1 medium onion, coarsely chopped

1 large shallot, coarsely chopped

3 cloves garlic, minced

1 tablespoon minced fresh ginger

1/2 to 1 tablespoon curry powder, to taste

2 cups water

Chutney Cream

1. Line a colander with cheesecloth, and place the yogurt in it to drain for a few hours, until thickened.

2. Chop the apple finely, and place it with the onion in a small saucepan. Add the ginger, vinegar, sweetener, and chili paste if desired. Bring to a boil, and simmer for 15 to 20 minutes, until thickened. Let cool.

3. Stir in the thickened yogurt. Set aside.

Pumpkin Soup

4. Heat the oven to 350°F.

5. Cut the tops off the pumpkins, and level the bottoms, if necessary, without cutting into the flesh too much. Scoop out the seeds and stringy pulp. Then cut and scrape out 4 cups of pumpkin flesh, being careful not to puncture the sides or bottom of the shells with the knife. Leave the walls thick enough so they won't collapse.

6. Place the pumpkin shells upside down in a large baking dish. Add water until it is 1/2 inch deep in the dish, and bake for about 35 minutes (if 1 large pumpkin, about 1 hour), until the flesh is tender but the shells still hold their shape. Check that the water doesn't evaporate and that the shells don't overcook.

7. While the shells are baking, chop the pumpkin flesh coarsely. Heat the oil in a large saucepan, and sauté the pumpkin flesh, onion, shallot, garlic, and ginger over low heat for 5 minutes.

Continued on page 56

2 tablespoons miso

2 cups buttermilk (or nonfat milk)

Salt and pepper to taste

2 tablespoons pomegranate seeds

18 cilantro leaves

8. In a small, dry sauté pan, toast the curry powder for 5 to 10 seconds. Then add it to the pumpkin mixture. Add the water and miso, and simmer for 15 to 20 minutes, until the vegetables are soft and the miso has dissolved.

9. Puree the mixture in a food processor, return it to the saucepan, add the buttermilk, and reheat. Season with the salt and pepper.

10. To serve, ladle the soup into the pumpkin shells. Place a dollop of chutney cream in the center of each. Sprinkle 1 teaspoon of pomegranate seeds and 3 cilantro leaves around the chutney. *

Roasted *Guajillo* and Garlic Chowder with Rosemary Sourdough Croutons

Tamara Frey

✷

This chowder uses *guajillo* chili paste, made from long, deep red chilies that are usually sold dried. They impart a full, fruity flavor to the soup. There are over 1,000 varieties of chili peppers. In this recipe you could substitute *ancho*, *pasilla*, or *chipotle* (for a smoky flavor).

Serves 6

Chowder

8 dried *guajillo* chilies (or any other dried chili)

2 bulbs garlic, unpeeled

1¹/₂ teaspoons corn oil

4 white potatoes, peeled and coarsely chopped

2 yellow onions, coarsely chopped

1 bay leaf

1 3- to 4-inch sprig thyme

1 cup white wine (such as chardonnay)

1 cup water

About 1¹/₂ cups milk
(or cream, nonfat milk, or soy milk)

Salt to taste

Croutons

1 cup fresh sourdough bread ¹/₂-inch cubes

1 teaspoon olive oil

1 teaspoon chopped fresh rosemary

1 tablespoon grated fresh Parmesan cheese

Chowder

1. Heat the oven to 500°F. Bring a large pot of water to a boil on the stove.

2. Roast the dried chilies in the oven for 30 seconds. Remove them, and reduce the oven heat to 350°F.

3. Simmer the chilies in the pot of water until they are very soft, about 20 minutes.

4. While the chilies simmer, rub the garlic bulbs with a little olive oil, and place them in a small baking dish. Roast them at 350°F for 45 minutes, or until they are soft. Set aside. Reduce the oven heat to 300°F for the croutons.

5. While the garlic is roasting, drain the chilies reserving a little of the cooking liquid. Remove the chili stems and seeds. Puree the chilies in a food processor, adding enough of the reserved liquid to form a paste. Set aside.

6. In a large stockpot, heat the corn oil. Sauté the potatoes and onions with the bay leaf and thyme over very low heat for about 8 minutes.

7. Add the wine, and deglaze the pot. Simmer for about 5 minutes to let the alcohol evaporate. Add the 1 cup of water, and simmer for 25 to 30 minutes, until the vegetables are soft.

8. Cut the tops off the roasted garlic bulbs, and squeeze the soft garlic cloves into the bowl of a food processor.

Continued on page 58

57

9. Using a slotted spoon, remove two-thirds of the potatoes and onions to the food processor, and puree with the garlic until smooth. Add the puree back to the stock containing the remaining vegetables.

10. Add all of but 1 teaspoon of the *guajillo* paste, the milk, and the salt to the chowder. Heat until just below the simmering point.

Croutons

11. In a medium bowl, toss the bread cubes with the olive oil and rosemary. Spread the cubes on a baking sheet, and bake at 300°F for about 20 minutes, turning often, until toasted. While they are still hot, toss them with the Parmesan.

12. To serve, ladle the chowder into bowls. Top each with a heaping tablespoon of croutons and make a swirl of the reserved *guajillo* paste on the side ✳

Cold Cucumber-Lime Soup

Tamara Frey

✳

The lime and mint in this soup cleanse the palate beautifully.

Serves 6

4 large cucumbers, peeled, seeded, and coarsely chopped

2 cups nonfat yogurt

1 1/2 cups buttermilk

2 1/2 tablespoons fresh mint, finely chopped

2 1/2 tablespoons fresh lime juice

Salt to taste

6 tablespoons julienned cucumber

6 sprigs mint

6 very thin slices lime

1. Puree the cucumbers in a food processor with the yogurt.

2. Pour the puree into a medium bowl, and whisk in the buttermilk. Add the chopped mint, lime juice, and salt.

3. Ladle into soup bowls, and garnish each serving with 1 tablespoon of julienned cucumber, a sprig of mint, and a slice of lime. ✳

Entrées

✵

Pork Tenderloin with Mango and Four-Pepper Sauce

Lars Kronmark

About 5 years ago I researched food from the Caribbean for a class, and I came across this dish.
I just love good pork dishes, especially those using tenderloins. The pork is so sweet and juicy here with
the Jamaica-inspired flavors, it is one of my new favorites.

Serves 4

1 large pork tenderloin, cut into 8 pieces
(about 2 ounces each)

1/2 teaspoon salt plus salt to taste

1/8 teaspoon each of ground allspice, nutmeg,
cayenne, and garlic powder

1/2 cup butter (or margarine)

2 tablespoons olive oil

3 cloves garlic, finely minced

1 small onion, thinly sliced

1 green, 1 red, and 1 yellow bell pepper, thinly sliced

1 teaspoon chopped jalapeño pepper
(with seeds if you like hot food)

1 mango (green is fine), peeled and sliced in strips

1 cup mango nectar (or papaya nectar)

Juice of 1 lime

Pepper to taste

2 tablespoons coarsely chopped cilantro

4 large sprigs cilantro for garnish (optional)

1. Flatten the pork pieces with the palm of your hand until they are about 1/2 inch thick.

2. In a small bowl, mix together the salt, allspice, nutmeg, cayenne, and garlic powder, and sprinkle half of the mixture on a large plate. Arrange the pork pieces on top, and sprinkle the other half of the seasonings over the pork.

3. In a large sauté pan or heavy skillet, heat 1/4 cup of the butter with the olive oil. Brown the pork quickly over high heat for about 2 minutes on each side. Then lower the heat, and let the meat cook slowly, uncovered, for about 5 minutes on each side.

4. While the pork is cooking, heat the remaining butter in a medium saucepan. Don't let it brown. Sauté the garlic for 1 minute, until it is transparent. Add the onion, bell peppers, jalapeño, and mango strips, and sauté for 3 to 4 minutes. Add the nectar, lime juice, salt to taste, and pepper. Toss in the chopped cilantro.

5. Pour the pepper sauce in the middle of a platter. Lift the pork tenderloins from the pan, and pat them dry with a kitchen towel. Place them on top of the sauce. Garnish with the large sprigs of cilantro, if you like. *

Carne Asada and Chili Calzone

Greg Tompkins

✳

This calzone has a nice "bite" due to the serrano chili. For a milder heat, substitute an Anaheim chili or use red or green bell pepper for no heat at all. For more heat, substitute a *habanero* chili, and mix a bit of your favorite hot sauce with the olive oil.

For an especially decadent dining experience, add bowls of guacamole and sour cream to serve with your bowl of dipping salsa.

Serves 2

1 recipe Cornmeal Pizza Dough
(recipe on page 115)

7 tablespoons olive oil

8 ounces thinly sliced *carne asada*
(flank steak)

8 ounces fresh (or thawed and drained
frozen) corn kernels

4 ounces shredded sharp cheddar cheese

2 serrano chilies, seeded and minced

2 teaspoons cumin seed,
toasted and ground

4 ounces shredded Monterey Jack cheese

Hot paprika (or New Mexico chili powder) to taste

½ cup *Salsa Verde* (recipe on page 188)

1. Heat the oven to 450°F.

2. On a lightly floured surface, press the pizza dough into 2 12-inch rounds. Brush them lightly with 4 tablespoons of the olive oil.

3. Lay the sliced *carne asada* evenly over half of each round. Cover the *carne asada* with the corn and cheddar. Sprinkle on the chilies and ground cumin, then cover the fillings with the Jack.

4. Fold the uncovered half of each round over the fillings, and seal the edges to form the "turnover" shape of calzone. Brush the tops of the calzone lightly with 2 tablespoons of the olive oil.

5. Bake for 20 minutes, until the crusts are a deep golden brown.

6. Remove the calzone from the oven, and brush them lightly with the remaining olive oil. Dust the tops lightly with the hot paprika. Cool the calzone on a rack, until they are eating temperature. Then slice, and serve with the salsa for dipping. ✳

Chicken Breasts Stuffed with Taleggio Cheese, Prosciutto, and Sage

Linda Carucci

This dish is very elegant and yet so simple to make. It's wonderful for a picnic, served chilled alone, or in a sandwich. For entertaining, the chicken breasts may be prepared in advance through step 4. Cover and refrigerate the stuffed breasts until 20 minutes prior to cooking. The sauce, too, can be prepared ahead, covered, and stored in the refrigerator for up to 3 days. Use it as a sandwich spread instead of mayonnaise.

Serves 4

4 boned half chicken breasts
(28 ounces), butterflied

8 fresh sage leaves

6 slices (2 ounces) taleggio cheese

6 slices (2 ounces) prosciutto

2 tablespoons olive oil

6 sun-dried tomatoes in oil (³/4 ounce),
drained and chopped into ¹/8-inch dice

1 cup Marinara Sauce
(recipe on page 180)

16 fresh basil leaves,
cut into chiffonade

1. Heat a grill.

2. Lay each butterflied breast flat, skin side down, between 2 pieces of plastic wrap, and pound until the breast is uniformly ¼ inch thick.

3. Place 2 leaves of the sage, 1½ slices of the cheese, and 1½ slices of the prosciutto, in that order, on half of each butterflied breast.

4. Fold the other half over, enclosing the layers, and secure with toothpicks. Brush both sides of the chicken with the olive oil.

5. Grill approximately 6 to 8 minutes on each side.

6. While the chicken is grilling, add the tomatoes to the Marinara Sauce, and heat in a small saucepan until hot. Stir in the basil.

7. To serve, spoon a fourth of the sauce on each of 4 plates, and place a grilled chicken breast on top. ✳

Grilled *Chipotle*-Citrus Quail

Dan Bowe

✳

Southwestern cuisine is not only flavorful but also low in fat. I particularly like this recipe because the flavors are so wonderfully intense and the marinade can also be used as a salad dressing.

Serves 4

6 cups Roasted Vegetable Stock
(recipe on page 185)

2 teaspoons cornstarch

1 cup lime juice

1 cup orange juice

1 teaspoon salt

2 *chipotle* chili peppers
(smoked, dried jalapeños), pureed
(or *chipotle* chili paste)

4 boneless quail

2 cups cooked white beans

1. In a small bowl, mix ½ cup of the stock with the cornstarch to form a slurry.

2. Bring the remaining vegetable stock to a boil in a large saucepan.

3. Add the cornstarch mixture, and stir until slightly thickened.

4. Remove the mixture from the heat, and allow it to cool.

5. In a large mixing bowl, combine the lime juice, orange juice, salt, and chili puree. Slowly whisk in the thickened, cooled vegetable stock.

6. Pour a fourth of the stock mixture into a large bowl or shallow dish. Add the quail, cover, and marinate in the refrigerator for 3 to 4 hours.

7. When you are ready to cook the quail, toss the cooked white beans with the remaining stock mixture in a small bowl.

8. Heat a grill, and grill the quail 3 to 4 minutes per side.

9. To serve, spoon a fourth of the beans onto each plate, and place the grilled quail on top of the beans. ✳

Summer Brochettes
with Orange-Ginger Marinade over Quinoa Pilaf

Tamara Frey

Quinoa comes from the high Andes of South America. This grain is a complete protein, delicious and easy to digest.

The marinade in this recipe uses Chinese hot bean paste (or chili paste). To make your own chili paste, puree any variety of dried chilies (stems and seeds removed) in a food processor with just enough toasted sesame oil to make a paste. Or soak a dried chili in hot water until it is soft, chop it finely, and add it to the marinade. This marinade is an all-time favorite, thick and flavorful.

Serves 4

Orange-Ginger Marinade

1 inch fresh ginger, peeled

3 large cloves garlic

1/4 to 1/2 teaspoon Chinese hot bean paste (or chili paste)

2 green onions

3/4 cup concentrated orange juice

3/4 cup sherry (dry or cream)

1/4 cup soy sauce

2 teaspoons toasted sesame oil

Brochettes

1 large sweet potato, peeled and cut into 1-inch cubes

2 red bell peppers, cut into 1-inch pieces

1 yellow bell pepper, cut into 1-inch pieces

1 medium red onion, cut into 1-inch cubes

8 medium shiitake mushrooms, cut into 1-inch pieces

1/2 pound shrimp (or scallops, shark, or swordfish, cut into 1-inch pieces)

Orange-Ginger Marinade

1. Puree the ginger, garlic, hot bean paste, and green onions together in a food processor.

2. Transfer the puree to a medium bowl, and add the orange juice, sherry, soy sauce, and sesame oil. Stir well. (Yield: about 2 cups.)

Brochettes

3. In a medium saucepan, cook the sweet potato cubes in simmering water just until al dente. Drain.

4. Skewer the vegetables and shrimp, alternating colors, shapes, and textures, on 8 skewers. Place them in a baking dish, and spoon the marinade over them, thoroughly coating each piece. Marinate, refrigerated, for 2 to 4 hours, turning and basting the skewers every hour or so. Meanwhile, prepare the pilaf and garnishes.

Quinoa Pilaf

5. Boil the water with the orange zest. Add the quinoa, and simmer, uncovered, until the liquid is absorbed, stirring now and then.

6. Add the green onions and parsley.

Continued on page 70

Quinoa Pilaf

5 cups water (or stock)

4 tablespoons orange zest

2 1/2 cups quinoa

3 green onions, minced

4 tablespoons minced parsley

Garnishes

2 teaspoons sesame seeds

4 green onions

8 orange "wheels" (crosswise slices)

Variation: Spicy Asian Marinade

1 1/2 teaspoons minced fresh ginger

1 1/2 teaspoons minced garlic

1 cup cream sherry

1/4 cup rice wine vinegar

1/4 cup water

1 teaspoon minced green onion

1/2 cup apple juice

2 tablespoons soy sauce

1/2 teaspoon Chinese hot bean paste (or to taste)

1 1/2 tablespoons arrowroot

1/2 teaspoon toasted sesame oil

Garnishes

7. In a hot, dry sauté pan, toast the sesame seeds over medium heat until lightly browned.

8. Trim the roots of the green onions. Cut off the green tops, and save for another use. Make several slits through the white part, leaving 1/2 inch intact at the base. Place in ice water for 15 minutes. The cut parts will fan out like a brush, making an impressive garnish.

9. Grill or broil the brochettes over a moderate flame, basting them frequently with the marinade.

10. Simmer the extra marinade until it has heated through and thickened, if necessary.

11. To serve, place a bed of quinoa pilaf on each plate. Lay 2 brochettes on the pilaf. Place a scallion brush decoratively beside the brochettes and an orange wheel on either side of the quinoa bed. Spoon the simmered marinade over the brochettes, and top with a sprinkling of toasted sesame seeds. ✳

Summer Brochettes can be made using Spicy Asian Marinade, instead of Orange-Ginger Marinade.

1. Whisk all the ingredients together, until there are no lumps in the arrowroot.

2. In a small saucepan, simmer the sauce until it thickens, stirring to prevent lumps from forming. Use as a marinade for the brochettes and a sauce to garnish them. (Yield: about 2 1/4 cups.) ✳

Thai Chicken Pizza

Greg Tompkins

I am never sure how much peanut sauce to use in this pizza, but I like more rather than less. I favor the House of Tsang brand.

You probably will have a very liquid mixture after you toss the bean sprouts with the rest of the ingredients. Either drain the mixture in a colander or squeeze every handful of topping lightly to remove excess liquid before you put it on the dough.

Serves 4

½ recipe Pizza Dough
(recipe on page 115)

1 tablespoon peanut oil

1 chicken breast, boned, skinned, and cut into ¼-inch dice

1 large carrot, coarsely shredded

1¼ cups Thai peanut sauce

4 ounces fresh bean sprouts

Chopped cilantro to taste

Chopped green onion to taste

Toasted sesame seeds to taste

1. If you have a pizza stone, place it in the oven. Heat the oven to 425°F.

2. Press the dough into a 12-inch round shape.

3. Heat a sauté pan or wok until very hot. Add the oil, and quickly parcook the chicken and carrot, stirring frequently, for 3 minutes (they will finish cooking in the oven). Add ¼ cup of the peanut sauce, and remove the pan from the heat. Add the bean sprouts, and toss the mixture to coat everything evenly.

4. Transfer the dough round to a pizza peel, pizza pan, or sheet pan. Place the chicken mixture evenly on the dough. Slide the pizza onto your pizza stone, or place the pan in the oven.

5. Bake the pizza for 12 to 15 minutes, until the crust is firm and lightly browned.

6. Remove the pizza from the oven, and sprinkle it with the cilantro, green onion, and sesame seeds. Cut into 8 slices, and serve with a bowl of the remaining peanut sauce. *

Chile Toreado con Camarones (Hot Chilies with Prawns)

Tamara Frey

✳

Whenever I make this recipe, I think of the beaches of Mexico and the warm summer nights when I first had this dish. Don't be afraid of the heat from the jalapeños, but, if you really want to avoid any heat at all, substitute an equal amount of green bell pepper.

Serves 6

5 tomatoes, cored

2 teaspoons sunflower oil

1 large white onion, cut into 1/8-inch strips

5 jalapeño peppers, trimmed, seeded, and cut into 1/8-inch strips

1/4 teaspoon salt

1 tablespoon rice vinegar

18 large (or jumbo) prawns, shelled and deveined

1/2 cup tequila

5 cloves garlic, minced

4 tablespoons chopped cilantro

4 teaspoons lime juice

Garnish

12 corn tortillas

1 avocado, cut into 12 wedges

6 lime wedges

Sunflower petals

1. Heat water in a medium saucepan. When it is simmering, dip the tomatoes in for 30 seconds. Drain the tomatoes, and slip off the skins. Cut the tomatoes in half crosswise, cup them in the palms of your hands, and squeeze out the seeds. Chop the tomatoes finely, and set them aside.

2. Heat a medium sauté pan. Add 1 teaspoon of the oil, and sauté the onion and jalapeño strips for 8 to 10 minutes, until they are soft. Add the salt and vinegar. Set aside.

3. While the onion and jalapeños are cooking, heat a large sauté pan. Add the remaining oil, and sauté the prawns for about 2 minutes on each side. When they turn a rosy sunrise pink, turn up the heat until the pan is quite hot. Remove the pan from the heat, pour in the tequila, and tilt the pan to catch the flame from the burner (or light the tequila with a match). Let the tequila cook until the alcohol burns off.

4. To the flambéed prawns, add the tomatoes, garlic, and cilantro. Sauté for about 2 minutes, until the flavors blend and the prawns are cooked through. Add the lime juice.

5. Dip the tortillas in water, and heat them on a dry griddle, turning often, until they are soft and heated through (or wrap them in aluminum foil and heat them in a 350°F oven for 5 minutes).

6. To serve, spoon 2 tablespoons of the onion and jalapeños on each plate. Arrange 3 prawns with the tomato sauce attractively on top. Garnish each plate with 2 avocado wedges, a lime wedge, 2 warm corn tortillas, and a few sunflower petals. ✳

Mexfest Crepes

Michael Kalanty

This dish was invented for the annual beachside Mexfest party I celebrate with my brothers and sisters. Originally, the filling included crabmeat and was wrapped in corn husks, more like a traditional Mexican tamale. In this simpler version, easily made crepes replace the difficult-to-find husks. To enhance the Mexican character of the dish, you can substitute ½ cup of finely ground cornmeal for an equal amount of all-purpose flour in the Basic Crepes recipe.

Serves 4

Shrimp Filling

24 medium shrimp, peeled and deveined (about 1 pound)

Juice of 1 lime

¼ teaspoon salt

2 tablespoons minced fresh cilantro

Corn Filling

3 quarts water

1½ teaspoons salt

3 teaspoons sugar

4 ears corn

18 cherry tomatoes, halved

¼ cup red wine vinegar

½ teaspoon freshly cracked black pepper

1 teaspoon Dijon mustard

¼ cup corn oil

¼ cup olive oil

8 Basic Crepes (recipe on page 143), made 8 inches wide

Shrimp Filling

1. Place the shrimp in a medium glass or ceramic bowl, and combine with the lime, salt, and cilantro. Toss to coat the shrimp evenly. Cover, and keep refrigerated until needed.

Corn Filling

2. In a large pot, boil the water with 1 teaspoon of the salt and 2 teaspoons of the sugar. Immerse the corn, and return to a boil. Cover the pot, turn off the heat, and let the corn sit for 5 minutes. Drain and cool the corn.

3. Cut the kernels from the corn, and place them in a medium bowl with the tomatoes.

4. In a small bowl, combine the vinegar, the remaining teaspoon of sugar, the remaining ½ teaspoon of salt, the pepper, and the mustard. Gradually whisk in the oils until well blended, and pour over the corn mixture. Toss to mix well. Add more salt if needed. Cover the bowl, and refrigerate until needed.

Crepes

5. Preheat the oven to 375°F. Line a baking tray with parchment.

6. To assemble, place the crepes browned side down. Place 3 shrimp in the center of each crepe. Place a mound of the corn mixture on top of the shrimp. Fold up the edges of the crepe to form a square. Carefully invert the crepes onto the baking tray.

7. Bake for 12 to 15 minutes, until the crepes are slightly crisp and the filling is heated through.

Tomatillo Sauce

½ cup finely chopped yellow onion

1 tablespoon corn oil

1 teaspoon minced garlic

1 12-ounce can tomatillos, drained
and finely chopped

1 jalapeño, halved, seeded,
and chopped

1 teaspoon sugar

½ teaspoon salt

⅓ cup sour cream

Fresh cilantro leaves

Tomatillo Sauce

8. While the crepes are baking, sauté the onion in the corn oil in a medium skillet over moderate heat. Add the gralic, and sauté for 15 seconds.

9. Add the tomatillos and jalapeño, and simmer for 5 minutes.

10. Add the sugar and salt, and simmer for 2 minutes more.

11. When the crepes are done, remove the tomatillo sauce from the heat.

12. To serve, place 2 crepes on each plate, and cover with the tomatillo sauce. Top with a dollop of sour cream and garnish with the cilantro leaves. *

Steamed Mussels and Clams

Louie Jocson

✳

I like to serve this dish because it's elegant, simple, and delicious.

Serves 4

½ cup olive oil

4 teaspoons minced garlic

4 tablespoons finely diced onion

4 tablespoons finely diced carrot

4 tablespoons finely diced celery

32 black mussels

32 littleneck clams

½ cup white wine

4 tablespoons coarsely chopped parsley

2 cups Basic Fish Stock (recipe on page 187)
(or clam juice)

1. Heat a large saucepan. Add the olive oil, and sauté the garlic, onion, carrot, and celery for 5 minutes, over medium heat, until the onion is translucent.

2. Add the mussels and clams. Stir.

3. Add the wine, parsley, and fish stock. Cover, and simmer for 10 minutes. Discard any mussels or clams that have not opened. ✳

Cioppino

Johnathan Robinette

*

A hearty seafood-and-tomato stew, cioppino began humbly in the North Beach district of San Francisco when Portuguese and Italian fishermen would "chip in" some of the fish from their day's catch to the community meal. It can be served with pasta, rice pilaf, or, in San Francisco style, in the hollowed-out center of a crisp, round loaf of sourdough bread.

Serves 10

¼ cup olive oil

1 medium onion, cut into medium dice

4 cloves garlic, minced

½ medium green pepper, cut into medium dice

½ bulb fennel (or 1 rib celery), cut into medium dice

4 medium tomatoes, peeled, seeded, and cut into medium dice

½ cup tomato juice

½ teaspoon dried red chili flakes

1 teaspoon fennel seed

½ cup chopped fresh basil

4 cups dry white wine

2 whole Dungeness crabs, cooked, cracked, and cleaned

1 pound sea scallops

¾ pound large prawns, peeled and deveined

14 large clams in their shells

1 pound boned, skinned white-fleshed fish, cut into 1-inch cubes

Salt to taste

½ cup loosely packed fresh parsley, coarsely chopped

10 sprigs fresh oregano

1. Place the olive oil in a large stockpot over medium heat, and add the onion and garlic. Cook for 4 minutes, until the onion is tender and translucent.

2. Turn the heat to high, and add the pepper, fennel, tomatoes, tomato juice, chili flakes, fennel seed, and basil. Cover, bring to a simmer, reduce the heat to medium low, and cook at a simmer for 12 minutes.

3. Add the wine, and layer the seafood in the pot, beginning with the crabs, then adding the scallops, prawns, clams, and fish. Cover and simmer for 8 to 10 minutes, until the fish cubes are tender and moist. Do not stir. Taste, and add salt if desired.

4. To serve, ladle the cioppino into large soup bowls, sprinkle with the parsley, and garnish with an oregano sprig. *

Baked Santa Barbara Shrimp

Louie Jocson

✻

This dish combines the wonderful flavors of shrimp and sea scallops. The recipe is great for entertaining, because you can prepare it through step 6 and hold it in the refrigerator until you're ready to bake it.

Serves 4

8 tablespoons olive oil

3/8 teaspoon Dijon mustard

4 teaspoons minced garlic

12 whole Santa Barbara shrimp (or jumbo shrimp with heads on), butterflied in the shell

Cracked black pepper to taste

12 sea scallops

1/2 cup chopped fresh fennel leaves

1/2 cup chopped fresh parsley

3/4 cup unsalted butter, softened

3/4 cup bread crumbs

1/2 cup grated Parmesan cheese

1.   Heat the oven to 450°F.

2.   In a small bowl, whisk together the oil, mustard, and garlic.

3.   Place the shrimp on a baking sheet. Brush them with the oil mixture, and season them with the pepper.

4.   Slice scallops in half horizontally, and place 2 halves side by side on each shrimp.

5.   In a small bowl, combine the fennel, parsley, and butter. Place 1 tablespooon of the mixture on top of each shrimp.

6.   Top with the bread crumbs and Parmesan.

7.   Bake for 15 to 18 minutes, until the shrimp flesh is firm to the touch. ✻

Red Snapper Basil Ragout

Lars Kronmark

If you like fish soups and stews and foods that are easy to eat, then here is what I call a real basic dish. It leaves you with options to add anything you like, from Thai spices to your favorite seafood. Be sure to serve it with sourdough bread.

Serves 4

2¹/₂ cups water

3 tablespoons lemon juice

¹/₂ cup orange juice

2 teaspoons grated orange zest

1 sprig sage

1 sprig parsley

2 bay leaves

Salt and pepper to taste

1¹/₂ cups clam juice

6 tablespoons olive oil

6 shallots, halved

1 bulb fennel, cut into ¹/₂-inch dice

1 carrot, cut into ¹/₂-inch dice

4 medium red potatoes,
cut into ¹/₂-inch dice

1 pound red snapper fillets,
cut into 1-inch cubes

¹/₂ bunch fresh basil (about 24 leaves)

1. In a 4-quart stockpot, combine the water, lemon juice, orange juice, orange zest, sage, parsley, and bay leaves. Simmer for 20 minutes. (The stock should not reduce by more than a third.) Season with the salt and pepper. Add the clam juice and 3 tablespoons of the olive oil. Set aside.

2. In a large frying pan with straight sides, heat the remaining 3 tablespoons of oil, and sweat the shallots, fennel, and carrot, covered, for 6 to 7 minutes, until the vegetables are soft.

3. Bring the stock to a boil again, add the potatoes, reduce the heat, and simmer for 6 minutes.

4. While the potatoes are cooking, add the snapper and basil to the frying pan, and cook over low heat for 2 minutes, tossing.

5. Add the boiling potato mixture to the frying pan, and stir to combine.

6. Serve immediately. *

Sautéed Sea Bass with Red Bell Pepper, Yellow Onion, and Thyme Seasoning

Dan Bowe

✳

When I first discovered using the pulp from my vegetable extractor, I couldn't believe how much flavor I was able to bring to food. You can experiment with other firm-fleshed fish as well as different combinations of flavoring agents.

Serves 2

2 tablespoons Extracted Vegetable Pulp Flavoring Agents (recipe on page 184), made half from red bell pepper and half from yellow onion

1 tablespoon chopped fresh thyme

1 1-pound fillet sea bass

Salt and pepper to taste

Nonstick vegetable spray

1. Mix the flavoring agents with the thyme, and spread the mixture on a tray.

2. Wash the fillet, and pat it dry.

3. Sprinkle the fillet with the salt and pepper. Then dredge it in the flavoring agent mixture, lightly pressing the mixture into the flesh of the fillet.

4. Spray both sides of the fillet with the nonstick spray.

5. Heat a medium sauté pan until hot. Place the fish in the pan, and sauté 3 to 5 minutes per side over medium heat, until cooked as you prefer. ✳

Grilled Monkfish Medallions
with Fennel-Olive-Tomato-Lemon Relish

Lars Kronmark

✳

It may be hard to get monkfish where you live, but ask for it or order it. The flesh is white, very juicy,
and meaty. I sure have cleaned my share of monkfish in Scandinavia. What an ugly fish to look at when cleaning!
But it is great for eating with a good bottle of dry white wine from the Sonoma coast.

The relish in this recipe can be chilled in the refrigerator before serving, but I like it best at room temperature.
The fennel is cooked in only a small amount of water so the flavor doesn't get lost.

Serves 4

Relish

2 cups water

1/2 teaspoon salt, plus salt to taste

1 4-ounce fennel root (or celery root)

2 Roma (or plum) tomatoes

8 black Kalamata (or other dry-cured) olives,
pitted and coarsely chopped

2 cloves garlic, minced

2 tablespoons capers (optional)

1 1/2 tablespoons lemon juice

1 tablespoon virgin olive oil

Freshly ground black pepper to taste

Medallions

2 monkfish fillets (8 to 9 ounces each)

4 thin slices lean bacon
(or pancetta, Italian bacon)

2 tablespoons olive oil

Salt and freshly ground black pepper to taste

Relish

1. In a small pot, bring the water and 1/2 teaspoon of salt to a boil.
    Add the fennel root whole, and cook for 10 to 15 minutes, until
    tender. Drain, and set aside to cool (or refrigerate).

2. Cut the tomatoes into quarters lengthwise, and remove the
    centers with the seeds. Chop the tomatoes coarsely.

3. Mince the fennel, and place it in a medium bowl. Add the
    olives, tomatoes, garlic, capers, lemon juice, olive oil, remaining
    salt, and pepper, and toss well to blend. Set aside.

Medallions

4. Heat a grill for at least 10 minutes.

5. Trim all black skin from the monkfish, and cut the fillets into
    8 equal pieces. Using your hand, flatten them to about 1 inch
    thick.

6. Cut the bacon in half lengthwise, and wrap each strip all the way
    around a piece of fish, using a toothpick to secure the ends.

7. Brush the fish on each side with the oil, season both sides with
    the salt and pepper, and grill the medallions for 4 to 5 minutes on
    each side, until firm to the touch.

8. To serve, place 2 medallions on a heated plate, and top with
    fennel relish. ✳

Trout in Grape Leaves with Apple-Grape-Mint Relish

Lars Kronmark

✳

I first made this trout dish up in the California Sierra Nevada mountains, where streams and lakes are full of rainbow trout.
However, I didn't trust my luck and brought 4 good-size fish from the restaurant, much to the amusement of my fishing companions.

This dish is really easy. Grape leaves are sold pickled in glass jars.
They make a tasty edible wrapper and keep the trout moist. Enjoy trout this way on a fishing trip if not at home.

Serves 4

Wrapped Trout

4 boneless trout

1/3 teaspoon salt

1/3 teaspoon pepper

1 lemon, cut crosswise into 8 slices

8 pickled grape leaves

1 tablespoon olive oil

2 shallots, finely diced

1 cup dry white wine

1 cup clam juice

Relish

1/3 cup red grapes, halved and seeded

1 medium green apple

1/2 small white onion, diced

8 mint leaves, chopped into chiffonade

1 tablespoon cider vinegar

1 tablespoon olive oil

1 teaspoon sugar

Pinch of salt

Pinch of pepper

4 whole mint leaves

Wrapped Trout

1. Heat the oven to 350°F.

2. Clean the trout in running water. Using scissors, cut off the fins, dry the fish with a kitchen towel, and salt and pepper the insides. Place 2 slices of lemon inside each trout cavity. Completely wrap each fish in 2 grape leaves.

3. Brush a flameproof, covered baking dish with the olive oil, and sprinkle the shallots in the bottom. Lay the wrapped trout on top, and pour the wine and clam juice over them. Cover the dish.

4. Bring the dish to a low simmer on the stove. Then place it immediately in the oven, and bake for about 12 minutes.

Relish

5. Place the grape halves in a medium bowl. Cut the apple, leaving the skin on, if you wish, into dice the size of the grape halves. Add the apple, onion, and chopped mint to the bowl, and toss with the vinegar, oil, sugar, salt, and pepper.

6. To serve, place a wrapped trout in the center of each plate. Spoon a fourth of the relish beside the trout, and garnish with a whole mint leaf. ✳

Seared Ahi Tuna with Sesame Seed and Black Peppercorn Crust on Asian Salad

Lars Kronmark

✳

In San Francisco I was introduced to another great style of cooking, Pacific Rim cuisine.
What great techniques and flavors, yet so simple! Enjoy the exotic world of this very "in" and timeless dish.

I think this salad goes very well with grilled chicken breast also.

Serves 4

Asian Salad

¹/₂ head Napa cabbage, cut into very fine strips

1 cup onion sprouts

1 small carrot, cut into fine strips (or grated)

4 green onions, cut into strips 2 inches long

1 clove garlic, minced

1 teaspoon minced jalapeño

1 tablespoon minced fresh ginger

¹/₄ cup fish sauce (or tamari sauce)

¹/₂ cup rice wine vinegar

Salt and pepper to taste

¹/₄ cup light corn syrup

Tuna

¹/₄ cup sesame seeds

2 tablespoons minced garlic

2 tablespoons minced fresh ginger

2¹/₂ pounds Ahi tuna loin

4 tablespoons cracked black peppercorns

2 tablespoons oil

Asian Salad

1. In a large bowl, toss the cabbage with the sprouts. Add the carrot strips and green onion strips.

2. In a small bowl, whisk together the garlic, jalapeño, ginger, fish sauce, vinegar, salt, and pepper. Whisk in the corn syrup.

3. Pour the dressing over the cabbage mixture, and toss. Set aside.

Tuna

4. In a small bowl, mix the sesame seeds, garlic, and ginger. Set aside.

5. Cut the tuna into 2-by-2-by-8-inch pieces.

6. Place the cracked pepper on a work surface. Press the pepper into the tuna on 2 opposite 8-inch sides.

7. Place the sesame seed mixture on a work surface. Press the mixture into the 2 remaining 8-inch sides of the tuna.

8. Heat a large sauté pan over high heat for 3 to 4 minutes. Add the oil, and swirl it around the pan.

9. Place the tuna in the hot pan, and cook over high heat for 3 minutes on each of the 4 coated sides.

10. Remove the tuna, and slice it into 8-by-2-by-¹/₂-inch slices.

11. Serve the slices on a bed of the Asian Salad. ✳

Country Cassoulet

Tamara Frey

✳

This "one-pot wonder" can be served as a family staple. The beauty of this dish is that any vegetable can be used. For example, try rutabaga, parsnips, or turnip in place of the sweet potato.

Serves 6

2 pounds potatoes (baby new, rosefir, or yellow fin), unpeeled (if young and tender), cut into 3/4-inch pieces

3/4 pound green and/or yellow beans, cut into 1/4-inch pieces

1/2 pound shiitake mushrooms, halved (or quartered if large)

1 cup sun-dried tomatoes

6 large cloves garlic

1 large sweet potato, peeled and cut into 3/4-inch pieces

3 baby beets, peeled and quartered

2 medium yellow onions, cut into 1/4-inch pieces

2 large carrots, cut into 1/4-inch pieces

1 pound asparagus, with woody ends snapped off

1 cup full-bodied red wine (such as zinfandel or petite sirah)

3/4 pound firm tofu (or chicken, swordfish, goat, etc.), cut into 1-inch cubes

2 tablespoons extra virgin olive oil

1/2 cup water

3 tablespoons soy sauce

1/2 teaspoon black pepper

3 4-inch sprigs fresh rosemary

3 bay leaves

1 loaf crusty onion-herb bread (or sourdough bread)

6 2-inch sprigs fresh rosemary

1. Adjust the oven rack to the middle of the oven. Heat the oven to 350°F.

2. Place all the vegetables except the asparagus in a heavy, deep, covered pot. Then add the wine, tofu, olive oil, water, soy sauce, pepper, 4-inch sprigs of rosemary, and bay leaves. Bake, covered, in the middle of the oven for 45 minutes. Stir well.

3. Add the asparagus, and bake for another 45 minutes, until the sauce is well developed and the vegetables are browned.

4. Serve in large dinner terrines, with slices of the crusty bread. Garnish each serving with a 2-inch rosemary sprig. ✳

Baked Stuffed Manicotti

Linda Carucci

*

My grandmother developed this recipe to utilize the fresh ricotta and mozzarella cheese my grandfather produced in their commercial dairy in Connecticut. The crepes may be stuffed and assembled in advance. Cover and refrigerate until 1 hour before baking.

Serves 8

Crepes

1 cup flour

1 cup water

3 eggs

Pinch salt

1 teaspoon salad oil
(plus oil for greasing the crepe pan)

Filling

1½ pounds whole-milk ricotta

2 eggs, lightly beaten

1 tablespoon chopped Italian parsley

3 tablespoons grated Romano (or Parmesan) cheese, plus more for garnish

½ teaspoon salt

¼ teaspoon pepper

¼ teaspoon sugar

½ pound whole-milk mozzarella, cut into ¼-inch dice

2 cups Marinara Sauce (recipe on page 180)

Crepes

1. Place all of the crepe ingredients (except the oil for the pan) into a bowl, and mix thoroughly until smoth. Place the batter in the refrigerator for at least 1 hour. (It can be refrigerated overnight.)

2. Spread a long sheet of waxed paper over a flat work surface near the stove.

3. Heat a 6-inch crepe pan or skillet over medium-high heat. Using a paper towel, rub about ¼ teaspoon of salad oil over the inside surface of the pan.

4. When the pan is hot, pour in 2 to 3 tablespoons of the crepe batter, and quickly lift and tilt the pan to distribute the batter evenly over the bottom of the pan. Return the pan to the burner, and cook just until the edges of the crepe start to curl and the center is dry to the touch.

5. Carefully invert the pan over the waxed paper, and tap the pan to release the crepe. The cooked side of the crepe should be light golden brown.

6. While the crepe is still warm, lift it from the waxed paper, to prevent it from sticking. Then place on the waxed paper again.

7. Repeat steps 3 through 6 with the remaining crepe batter, placing the crepes side by side on the waxed paper. (Yield: About 16 crepes.)

Filling

8. Pour off and discard any liquid from the top of the ricotta in its container. Place the ricotta in a large mixing bowl with the eggs, parsley, Romano, salt, pepper, and sugar. Whisk the ingredients together just until combined.

9. Add half of the mozzarella to the ricotta mixture, and stir just until combined. (If you are not filling the crepes immediately, refrigerate the filling mixture until ready to use.)

10. Heat the oven to 325°F. Butter a 9-by-13-inch casserole dish.

11. Distribute the remaining half of the mozzarella among the crepes in a strip down the center of each crepe. (Check that each crepe separates easily from the waxed paper. A blunt table knife may be helpful.)

12. Divide the filling equally among the crepes, covering the strips of mozzarella.

13. Lift one side of each crepe, and fold it over the strip of filling. Fold over the opposite side, forming a cylinder. Carefully transfer each rolled crepe to the casserole dish, seam side down, lining the manicotti up close to each other.

14. Cover the manicotti with a light layer of the Marinara Sauce. Reserve the rest of the sauce.

15. Bake for 20 to 30 minutes, until bubbles appear in the center of the casserole dish.

16. Remove from the oven, and let stand for 5 minutes. Sprinkle with some grated Romano before serving.

17. Serve 2 manicotti per person, and pass the remaining Marinara Sauce. Store leftover manicotti in the refrigerator. ✳

Leek and Anaheim Chili Custard with Chili Salsa and *Habanero* Cornbread

Tamara Frey

✳

Chili peppers have been on earth for about 10,000 years. The distinct flavor and fire of the *habanero* chili pepper in the cornbread here complements perfectly the mild custard.

Be careful when handling chilies; the heat stays on your hands and can irritate your eyes if you touch them.

Serves 4

Custard

2 large fresh Anaheim chilies
(or about 1 cup chopped canned)

1 teaspoon sunflower oil
(or corn oil)

$1/2$ leek, minced

$1/2$ red bell pepper, minced

2 tablespoons white wine
(such as sauvignon blanc)

4 eggs

4 tablespoons cream

Salt and pepper to taste

2 teaspoons chopped fresh oregano

2 tablespoons crumbled *queso fresco*
(or feta cheese)

Habanero Cornbread

$1 1/4$ cups cornmeal

$1 1/4$ cups whole-wheat (or white) pastry flour

$1 1/4$ teaspoons ground cumin

2 teaspoons baking powder

Custard

1. Heat the oven to 350°F. Butter 4 4-ounce ramekins or custard cups.

2. Roast the Anaheim chilies over an open flame until their skins are charred. Enclose them in a paper bag for 8 to 10 minutes, shaking the bag now and then. Remove the peppers, and wash them under cool water until the skins slip off. Remove the stems and seeds, leaving the chilies whole.

3. Heat the sunflower oil in a medium sauté pan, and sauté the leek and bell pepper for 3 to 5 minutes. Place the whole Anaheims on top of the leek and pepper, add the wine, cover the pan, and steam the vegetables for 5 minutes, until the Anaheim peppers are thoroughly cooked.

4. Remove the Anaheims, and chop them coarsely. Place them in a food processor. Add the eggs and cream, and puree.

5. Transfer the puree to a bowl, and add the salt, pepper, oregano, and *queso fresco*. Add the cooked leek and bell pepper to the mixture.

6. Fill the prepared ramekins two-thirds full with the custard mixture. Bake in a bain-marie, covered with aluminum foil, for 35 minutes, until firm in the center.

Habanero Cornbread

7. Heat the oven to 350°F if not already at that temperature. Oil an 8-by-8-inch baking pan.

1 tablespoon chopped fresh oregano

1 tablespoon chopped fresh cilantro

2 tablespoons minced onion

1/2 teaspoon salt

1 tablespoon minced *habanero*
(or jalapeño) chili pepper

1 cup nonfat (or soy) milk

1 tablespoon maple syrup

2 tablespoons corn oil

1 egg

Salsa

1 dried *chile de árbol* (tree chili)

3 medium to large tomatoes, cored

1/2 teaspoon sunflower oil
(or corn oil)

2 tablespoons minced yellow (or white) onion

2 large cloves garlic, minced

2 tablespoons chopped fresh cilantro

8. Mix the cornmeal, flour, cumin, baking powder, oregano, cilantro, onion, salt, and *habanero* pepper together in a medium bowl.

9. Form a well in the cornmeal mixture, and add the milk, maple syrup, oil, and egg. Stir just until the dry ingredients are moistened, and pour into the oiled pan.

10. Bake for 20 to 30 minutes, until golden brown on top. Unmold from the pan, and cut diagonally into diamond-shaped pieces.

Salsa

11. While the cornbread is baking, make the salsa. In a medium saucepan of water, simmer the *chile de árbol* for about 10 minutes, until soft. Remove with a slotted spoon, chop finely, and set aside.

12. To the same pan of water add the tomatoes, simmer for about 30 seconds, remove with a slotted spoon, and slip off the skins. Cut the tomatoes in half crosswise, and, holding the halves in your palms, squeeze out the seeds. Chop the tomatoes finely, and set aside.

13. In a medium sauté pan, heat the oil, and sweat the onion and garlic. Add the tomato pulp and *chile de árbol*. Cook for 5 to 10 minutes to reduce the liquid, and add the cilantro.

14. To serve, spread 2 tablespoons of the salsa on each plate. Unmold a custard onto the salsa, and top the custard with a dollop of salsa. Place a cornbread diamond at the side. ✳

Caramelized Onion and White Cheddar Soufflé with Stout

Greg Tompkins

✳

This is the classic English pub soufflé (just kidding). It is unusual in that the base is made with stout (I prefer Guinness) instead of milk. The bitter stout marries well with the sweet caramelized onions and the simultaneously sharp and mellow cheddar.

Serves 4

1 large yellow onion, finely chopped

3 teaspoons oil

6 green onions, finely chopped

½ teaspoon sugar

1 teaspoon salt

¼ teaspoon pepper

2 cups stout

4 tablespoons butter

4 tablespoons flour

Pinch nutmeg

5 egg yolks

½ cup shredded white cheddar

6 egg whites

1. Heat the oven to 350°F. Thoroughly butter a 2-quart soufflé dish.

2. In a medium sauté pan over medium-low heat, cook the yellow onion in the oil until the pieces are caramelized (soft and brown).

3. Stir in the green onions.

4. In a small bowl, combine the sugar, salt, pepper, and stout. Stir to dissolve the salt and sugar. Pour the stout mixture over the onions, and set the pan aside.

5. Melt the butter in a medium sauté pan over medium heat. Stir in the flour to make a smooth paste, and cook the paste (roux), stirring frequently, for 3 to 5 minutes. Reduce the heat, if necessary, so you do not let the roux color.

6. Stir in the nutmeg, and gradually add the stout mixture, stirring constantly, until the base (of the soufflé) is thick and smooth. Remove from the heat.

7. Beat the egg yolks into the base until they are well incorporated, then fold in the cheddar. (The base may be cooled and refrigerated for up to 2 days at this point.)

8. Beat the egg whites until they form stiff (but not dry) peaks. Fold a fourth of the whites into the base, to loosen it. Then fold in the remainder of the whites.

9. Pour the batter into the prepared soufflé dish. Bake the soufflé in the lower third of the oven for 30 minutes, until it is well puffed and golden brown. Serve immediately. ✳

Variation: Individual Soufflés in Potato Shells

This soufflé can serve as a side dish, baked in hollowed-out baking potato shells. Bake 4 large russet potatoes at 350°F for 50 minutes. Split them in half lengthwise, and scoop the potato out of the shells, reserving the scooped potato for another use. Spoon or pipe the soufflé mixture into the potato shells, and bake them in a 400°F oven for 20 to 25 minutes. Serve immediately.

Variation: Ham, Cheese, and Onion Soufflé

Fold ⅓ cup finely diced dry-cured ham (such as Smithfield or prosciutto) into the soufflé base with the cheese. This version is like a ham and cheese sandwich and a beer all in one soufflé.

Soufflé Roulade

Greg Tompkins

This recipe should dispel any notion you have of soufflés as fragile and delicate. Here the soufflé is baked on a cookie sheet, allowed to fall, then filled and rolled. Slicing the resulting "jelly roll" into disks and on the bias allows for a spectacular presentation.

Serves 12

Soufflé Roll

4 tablespoons butter

2 teaspoons Dijon mustard

Salt, pepper, cayenne, and nutmeg to taste

¼ cup flour

2¼ cups milk

¼ cup plus 3 tablespoons grated Parmesan cheese

1¼ cups grated fontina cheese

10 egg yolks

10 egg whites

Filling

1 tablespoon olive oil

1 cup diced red bell peppers, in ¼-inch pieces

2 tablespoons sliced green onions, in ¼-inch rounds

1 pound fresh spinach

1 cup bay shrimp

2⅛ cups Extracted Red Pepper Juice Sauce (recipe on page 183)

Soufflé Roll

1. Melt the butter in a medium saucepan. Add the mustard, salt, pepper, cayenne, and nutmeg. Add the flour, and whisk to combine. Cook for 3 to 5 minutes, over medium heat, whisking frequently. Add the milk, and whisk over medium heat for about 5 minutes, until thickened. Remove from the heat, and cool the white sauce for 30 minutes, until room temperature.

2. When the sauce has cooled, heat the oven to 425°F. Line a sheet pan with parchment paper, and grease the paper with butter.

3. Set aside ½ cup of the white sauce (for the filling), and pour the rest into a medium mixing bowl. Add the ¼ cup of Parmesan and the fontina, and mix thoroughly. Then add the egg yolks, and incorporate fully.

4. In a large bowl, whisk the egg whites until they form stiff peaks. Stir a third of the egg whites into the cheese mixture. Fold in the remaining two-thirds of the egg whites.

5. Pour the soufflé onto the prepared sheet pan, spreading the mixture evenly. Bake it for 15 to 18 minutes, until the soufflé has risen.

6. While the soufflé is baking, spread a piece of parchment on a work surface, and dust it with the 3 tablespoons of Parmesan.

7. When the soufflé has risen, remove it from the oven, and allow it to cool enough to handle. (The soufflé will fall.) Loosen it from the sides of the pan, and invert it onto the Parmesan-dusted parchment.

8. Peel the baking parchment from the soufflé, and replace it with a new piece of parchment. Roll the soufflé and parchment papers above and below it into a loose log, starting from a long edge. (The paper will keep the soufflé from sticking to itself.) Allow it to cool to room temperature, so that it will retain its shape.

Filling

9. Heat the olive oil in a medium sauté pan. Add the red peppers and green onions, and sauté for 3 minutes, until slightly softened. Add the spinach, cover, reduce the heat, and cook for another 3 to 5 minutes, until the spinach has wilted. Remove the lid, and stir the ingredients. Add the bay shrimp and the 1/2 cup of white sauce reserved from the soufflé roll. Stir to combine thoroughly. Remove from the heat, and cool to room temperature.

10. While the filling is cooling, line a sheet pan with aluminum foil. If you plan to serve the soufflé soon, heat the oven to 350°F.

11. Unroll the soufflé, remove the top parchment, and spread the filling evenly over the soufflé. Roll the soufflé again lengthwise, without the bottom parchment. Transfer the roulade to the foil-lined sheet pan, and wrap it in the foil. Either refrigerate it until you are ready to proceed or bake it for 20 minutes, until it is heated through.

12. To serve, slice the roulade into 3/4-inch slices. Line 12 plates with the Extracted Red Pepper Juice Sauce, and place 2 slices of roulade, cut side up, on each plate. ✳

Artichoke and Mushroom Risotto
with Asiago Cheese and Sun-Dried Tomatoes

Linda Carucci

✳

This recipe adds the distinctive California taste of artichokes and sun-dried tomatoes to the classic risotto, a traditional
rice dish of Italy. A delicious vegetarian entrée, it is also a perfect complement to grilled meat, fish, or poultry.

Serves 8

3 tablespoons olive oil

3 tablespoons butter

½ cup diced onion

2 cups finely chopped wild (or white) mushrooms

2 tablespoons minced garlic

2 cups Arborio rice

6 to 8 cups Light Vegetable Stock
(recipe on page 185)

1 cup dry white wine

14 to 16 artichoke hearts,
cooked and cut in half

¼ cup julienned sun-dried tomatoes

¾ cup finely grated Asiago cheese

8 pieces grilled garlic bread

1. In a 2-quart saucepan, heat the olive oil and butter over moderate heat. Add the onion, and cook until tender but not browned.

2. Add the mushrooms, and cook for 4 minutes more.

3. Add the garlic and rice, and cook for 2 minutes more, stirring to sauté the garlic lightly and coat the rice grains with oil.

4. In another saucepan, bring the stock to a simmer over low heat.

5. Add the wine to the rice mixture, and stir until the wine is almost completely absorbed.

6. Add a ladleful of the stock to the rice mixture, and bring to a simmer, stirring constantly. Once the rice has absorbed the stock, add the remaining stock in ½-cup increments, stirring until the rice has absorbed the liquid before each addition.

7. After 5 minutes, transfer the artichoke hearts to the simmering stock to infuse and warm them.

8. Continue adding stock in increments to the rice, including the artichoke hearts and the sun-dried tomatoes with the last addition of stock. As you stir, the artichokes will break apart. Cook the rice for a total of 15 to 20 minutes, until the risotto is soft but still firm to the tooth.

9. Stir in most of the Asiago cheese.

10. Transfer to a serving bowl, and sprinkle the remaining cheese on top. Serve immediately with the garlic bread. ✳

Galette of Potato and Celery Root

Michael Kalanty

A humble casserole, inspired by the classic Lyonnaise pairing of these root vegetables, is turned into an elegant and impressive buffet dish with the addition of a puff pastry topping. The galette can be baked ahead, cooled, and sliced into portions. Cover it lightly with aluminum foil, and heat in a 350°F oven for 30 to 40 minutes before serving.

Serves 6 to 8

8 ounces frozen puff pastry dough, defrosted in refrigerator

2 tablespoons unsalted butter

1 bay leaf

1 cup sliced yellow onions

3 cloves garlic, minced

1 cup heavy cream

1/2 cup plus about 1 tablespoon milk

1 teaspoon salt plus salt to taste

1/2 teaspoon freshly cracked black pepper, plus pepper to taste

2 pounds baking potatoes

1 celery root (about 3/4 pound), peeled and sliced 1/8 inch thick

1 tablespoon minced Italian parsley

1. On a lightly floured work surface, roll the puff pastry dough into a circle 1/8 inch thick and more than 11 inches in diameter. Place it on a baking tray, and refrigerate it for 20 minutes.

2. Adjust the oven rack to the middle of the oven. Heat the oven to 425°F. Butter a 10-inch deep-dish pie pan with 1 tablespoon of the butter, and set aside. Line a baking tray with parchment paper.

3. In a medium saucepan, heat the remaining tablespoon of butter with the bay leaf. Add the onions, and cook over low heat, tossing occasionally, for about 10 minutes, until onions are translucent.

4. Add the garlic and cook for 30 seconds. Carefully add the cream and the 1/2 cup of milk. Bring to a simmer. Season with the 1 teaspoon of salt and 1/4 teaspoon of the pepper. Remove from the stove, and cool to room temperature.

5. Peel the potatoes, and slice them 1/8 inch thick. Place half of them in a layer over the bottom of the prepared pie pan.

6. Drain the onion mixture, reserving the cream sauce. Discard the bay leaf. Scatter the onions and garlic over the layer of potatoes. Pour some cream sauce into the pie pan just to cover the potatoes.

7. Place the celery root in a layer over the potatoes. Season with some of the salt and the remaining 1/4 teaspoon of pepper.

8. Place the remaining potatoes over the celery root. Season with the salt to taste, and pour enough cream sauce into the pan to come almost to the top of the potato layer. Cover the pie pan tightly with aluminum foil.

9. Place the pan on the parchment-lined baking tray. Bake for 15 minutes, reduce the oven temperature to 375°F, and bake for 20 minutes more. Remove the galette from the oven, and allow it to cool for 5 minutes. Carefully remove the aluminum foil.

10. While the galette is baking, cut out an 11-inch circle of puff pastry dough. Brush the edge of the dough with water, and fold over a ½-inch border. Dip a fork in flour, and press down on the dough to seal the edges. Dock all over with a fork. Refrigerate on the tray until needed.

11. When the galette has rested 5 minutes, transfer the shaped dough, seam side down, to the pie pan, covering the potato mixture. Lightly tuck the dough around the potatoes.

12. Brush the dough lightly with the remaining tablespoon of milk, and return it to the oven. Continue to bake for 25 to 30 minutes, until the potatoes are tender and the crust is crisp. If the crust starts to become too brown while baking, place a piece of parchment paper over the top.

13. Remove from the oven, and cool on a rack for 15 minutes. Cut into slices, and serve, garnished with the parsley. ✳

Breads

✦

Herbed Garlic *Bâtards*

Greg Tompkins

Herbes de Provence is a traditional mixture of herbs used in southern France. Depending on who tells you of the tradition, the blend may have a few as 5 herbs or as many as 13.

For a lower-fat loaf, omit the ¼ cup of olive oil, and just use the single tablespoon for toasting the garlic.

2 bulbs garlic,
separated into unpeeled cloves

1 tablespoon plus ¼ cup olive oil

2¾ cups water

9¾ cups bread flour

2½ tablespoons malt

¼ cup *herbes de Provence*

2 packages rapid-rise yeast

5 teaspoons salt

1. Heat the oven to 350°F.

2. Toss the garlic cloves with the 1 tablespoon of oil in a small shallow roasting pan. Cover the pan tightly with aluminum foil, and roast for 70 to 90 minutes.

3. Let the cloves cool until they can be handled. Then squeeze each one to release the soft garlic inside into a small bowl. Discard the skins.

4. Add the water and remaining ¼ cup of olive oil to the garlic and stir to combine. Set aside.

5. In the large bowl of a mixer fitted with a dough hook, combine the rest of the ingredients, and stir lightly to blend. With the mixer on low speed, add the garlic mixture, and knead until the ingredients are moistened.

6. Switch to medium speed, and knead 10 to 12 minutes, until the dough is smooth and elastic. Add flour or water, as needed, to adjust the dough.

7. Allow the dough to rise in a warm place for 30 to 45 minutes, until it has doubled. Punch the dough down, and divide it into 3 pieces.

8. Form the dough into *bâtards:* Pound each piece of dough into a flat circle. Roll one edge halfway toward the center. Fold the two side edges over the rolled edge, and finish rolling to seal in the sides. Pinch the seam edges together to seal the loaf. Roll the loaf into a cylinder about 8 inches long. With one hand on each end of the loaf, roll the loaf toward you, pressing your fingers on the ends to taper the ends of the loaf. Repeat this as many times as it takes to form a smooth loaf that is thick in the center with tapered, almost pointed, ends, like a large yam or a football.

9. Allow the *bâtards* to rise for about 30 minutes, until they are half again as large.

10. While the *bâtards* are rising, set a pizza stone on the lowest rack or the bottom of the oven. Heat the oven to 500°F.

11. Place a shallow pan of boiling water on an upper rack in the oven. Slash the *bâtards* along their length. Place them on the pizza stone. Reduce the oven heat to 400°F. Bake the loaves for 10 minutes, then remove the pan of water, and continue baking the loaves for 15 to 20 minutes, until they sound hollow when tapped sharply on the bottom.

12. Cool the loaves slightly on a rack before slicing. (Yield: 3 1½-pound *bâtard* loaves.) ✳

Vanilla Challah

Greg Tompkins

Challah is the traditional bread of the Jewish Sabbath. It is not usually flavored with vanilla, however. To prepare this recipe without that flavoring, omit the vanilla beans and replace the vanilla sugar with regular granulated or brown sugar.

The three-braid is the generic form for a Sabbath challah. Other holy days have their own forms of challah, as varied as the events being celebrated.

The egg wash used here gives the challah a deep golden brown crust. For a darker crust, substitute milk or half-and-half for the water in the egg wash. The darker egg wash may also be used as a dip for slices of challah when making French toast.

This recipe is kosher. To make it pareve as well, replace the milk with water and the butter with vegetable oil.

2 vanilla beans

2 3/4 cups milk

1/3 cup Vanilla Sugar
(recipe on page 107)

10 cups bread flour

2 packages rapid-rise yeast

1 1/2 teaspoons salt

5 eggs

1/2 cup (1 stick) butter, softened

2 tablespoons water

1. Cut the tips off the vanilla beans. Using the point of a sharp knife, cut through the husk of the bean lengthwise, on one side only (don't cut the bean in half). Spread the bean open along the incision and, using the edge of the knife blade, scrape the inside of the bean from end to end several times, to extract as many of the fine vanilla seeds as possible. Gather the seeds, the scraped husk, and the tips of the beans in a medium saucepan.

2. Add the milk and vanilla sugar, and bring to a simmer. Remove the pan from the heat, and allow to steep until the milk is lukewarm. Strain the mixture, reserving the vanilla seeds, husk scrapings, and tips to make another batch of vanilla sugar.

3. In the large bowl of a mixer fitted with a dough hook, combine the flour, yeast, and salt, and stir lightly to blend.

4. Add the milk mixture, and knead at low speed until the milk is absorbed.

5. Beat 4 of the eggs together lightly, and add them to the moistened flour. Knead until the eggs are incorporated.

6. Add the butter, increase the mixer speed to medium, and knead for 12 minutes, until the dough is soft and smooth. Add flour or milk if needed to adjust the consistency of the dough.

7. Remove the dough from the bowl, and divide it into 8 pieces.

8. Allow the pieces to proof, covered, on a work surface until they have doubled in size. Then roll each piece into a tapered strand, and braid 3 strands together to make 2 loaves. Twist the remaining 2 strands together to make 1 twisted loaf. Turn the ends under, and press to seal them. Place the loaves on a baking sheet.

9. In a medium bowl, beat the remaining egg with the water. Brush the loaves with this egg wash. Allow each loaf to rise, covered, until half again as large.

10. Heat the oven to 350°F.

11. Bake for 20 to 30 minutes, until the loaves are a deep golden brown. Allow the challah to cool before slicing. (Yield: 2 3-braid loaves and 1 2-braid twist loaf.) *

Vanilla Sugar

2 vanilla beans

2 cups sugar

Follow step 1 of the main recipe, but instead of gathering the vanilla seeds, husk scrapings, and tips in a saucepan, bury them in the sugar for at least 1 week. They will perfume the sugar with the scent and flavor of vanilla. (Yield: 2 cups.) *

Santa Fe Chili-Cheese Roll-Ins

Greg Tompkins

The final shape of these rolls is determined by how tightly the dough sheet is rolled
into a cylinder after the filling is spread on it (see step 6).

For a bread with less heat, substitute Anaheim chilies or green bell pepper for the jalapeños.

Serves 12

Dry Ingredients

$1/2$ cup fine cornmeal

$7^1/2$ cups bread flour

$1/2$ cup sugar

$1/2$ tablespoon paprika

$1/2$ tablespoon toasted cumin seed

$1/2$ tablespoon ground cumin

$1/2$ tablespoon garlic powder

2 packages rapid-rise yeast

$1^1/2$ teaspoons garlic salt

Wet Ingredients

6 tablespoons olive oil

$3/4$ cup hot water

$1^1/2$ cups buttermilk,
at room temperature

1 egg

1. In the large bowl of a mixer fitted with a dough hook, whisk together the dry ingredients.

2. In a medium bowl, whisk together the wet ingredients.

3. With the mixer on low speed, add the wet ingredients to the dry ingredients, until they are moistened. Switch the mixer to medium speed, and knead for 8 to 10 minutes, adding flour or water if necessary to make the dough smooth and elastic.

4. Remove the dough from the mixer, and allow it to rest, covered, on a floured work surface for 30 minutes.

5. Roll the dough into a rectangle about $1/2$ inch thick.

6. Brush the rectangle with some of the egg wash. Then sprinkle the corn, jalapeños, and cheddar over it. Beginning on a long edge, roll the rectangle toward you into a cylinder (like a jelly roll). If you roll it tightly, expansion in the oven will force the center of each roll upward into an attractive peak. If you roll it loosely, expansion will push each layer outward to make rolls like oversized cinnamon rolls. Carefully seal the seam by pinching the dough together. The rolled dough cylinder should be about 4 inches in diameter. If it is larger, roll the sealed cylinder back and forth, as if you were rolling out a baguette, until the proper diameter is reached.

7. Heat the oven to 325°F. Line a baking sheet with parchment paper.

8. Cut the dough cylinder into 3-inch lengths, and place the pieces cut side up, staggered, on the baking sheet. With the palm of your hand, flatten each piece to $1^1/2$ to 2 inches high.

Filling

1 egg, lightly beaten, for wash

2 cups corn kernels (fresh or frozen)

1/3 cup minced jalapeño chilies

2 1/2 cups shredded sharp cheddar cheese

2 tablespoons butter

1/4 teaspoon minced garlic

9. Allow the pieces to rise until half again as large, and brush them with the remaining egg wash.

10. Bake for 20 to 30 minutes, until the rolls are golden.

11. While the rolls are baking, melt the butter in a small saucepan. Add the garlic, remove from the heat, and let steep for at least 5 minutes.

12. When the rolls are done, remove them from the oven, and brush them immediately with the garlic butter. ∗

Grissini
(Italian Bread Sticks)

Louie Jocson
✳

These bread sticks have a wonderful Parmesan flavor. If you ever have any left over, break them into 1/4-inch pieces and use them the next day as croutons in soup.

1/3 cup active dry yeast

1/4 cup sugar

2 tablespoons salt

1 quart lukewarm water

1 cup grated Parmesan cheese

3 tablespoons extra virgin olive oil

About 7 1/2 cups high-gluten bread flour

1. In a large electric mixer bowl, dissolve the yeast, sugar, and salt in the water.

2. Add the cheese and oil, and mix with a dough hook at low speed until combined.

3. Add the flour slowly until a dough forms.

4. Mix until the dough starts to pull away from the bowl and form a firm, stretchy ball. If the dough is still sticky, mix in small amounts of flour to achieve the correct consistency.

5. Cover the bowl, and let the dough rise in a warm place until it doubles in volume.

6. Punch the dough down, transfer it to a lightly floured work surface, and roll it out to a rectangle about 1/4 inch thick, 12 inches high, and as wide as it will go.

7. With a pizza cutter, cut strips 1/4 inch by 12 inches, and place them a little apart on a sheet pan.

8. Place the pan in a warm place for 15 to 20 minutes, until the strips are half again their original size.

9. Heat the oven to 350°F.

10. Bake for 12 to 15 minutes, until the *grissini* are golden brown, dry, and crisp.

11. Cool completely before serving. (Yield: 25 to 30 bread sticks.) ✳

Fennel *Focaccini*

Linda Carucci

✳

I came across this focaccia roll a few years ago in Southern California and have since
enjoyed several variations of it. I recently encountered it again when visiting restaurants in
the Northern California wine country. This version is inspired by Chef Ralph Tingle.

1 cup warm water (105°F to 115°F)

1 (¼-ounce) package active dry yeast

1 teaspoon sugar

1 tablespoon fennel seed

3¼ cups flour

1 teaspoon salt

1 tablespoon olive oil

1 tablespoon Ricard (anise-flavored liqueur)

Egg wash made with 1 egg
and 1 tablespoon water (optional)

1 tablespoon extra virgin olive oil

¾ teaspoon kosher salt

1. Measure ½ cup of the warm water into a warm, clear glass bowl. Sprinkle the yeast and sugar onto the water. Stir with a fork, and let the mixture stand 10 to 15 minutes, until it becomes foamy.

2. Heat a small nonstick skillet over medium heat. When the skillet is hot, add the fennel seed. Swirl the pan constantly to toast the seeds evenly. As soon as the seeds give forth an aroma and begin to turn brown, pour them into a large mixing bowl.

3. Add the flour and 1 teaspoon salt to the fennel seed, and stir together. Add the remaining ½ cup warm water, the olive oil, and the Ricard. Incorporate all ingredients by stirring with a wooden spoon.

4. Knead the dough for 10 minutes. If the dough sticks to your hands, add a little flour, but avoid adding too much flour.

5. Place the dough in a greased bowl, cover with plastic wrap, and set aside in a warm place to rise for 45 to 60 minutes, until the dough has doubled in bulk.

6. Heat the oven to 500°F.

7. Divide the dough into 24 pieces. Roll each piece into a ball the size of a golf ball, and place on a baking sheet. If desired, lightly brush the top of each ball with the egg wash. Bake for about 10 minutes, until the *focaccini* are golden brown.

8. Place the extra virgin olive oil in a large bowl. Transfer the baked *focaccini* to the bowl, and toss them in the olive oil. When they are evenly coated, sprinkle on the kosher salt. Serve immediately. (Yield: 2 dozen.) ✳

Focaccia

Greg Tompkins
✳

This version of the classic Italian bread was given to me by Chef Peter Teimorabadi, Senior Pastry Chef at the California Culinary Academy. It uses a predough and main dough. It is important to knead the predough until well developed, so that it will not rise and fall too quickly. When you cover the bowl, don't let the wrap touch the predough or it will artificially support the dough and you won't be able to tell when the dough has fallen.

Serves 16

Predough

5 ounces water

2 packages rapid-rise yeast

2 teaspoons sugar

2 cups bread flour,
plus additional flour if needed

Main Dough

5 cups bread flour

1/3 cup sugar

3/4 cup extra virgin olive oil

2 cups water

2 tablespoons olive oil

10 tablespoons Herbed Oil
(recipe on page 114)

2 tablespoons sea salt

Predough

1. Blend the first 3 ingredients of the predough in a mixer with a dough hook until the yeast is well dispersed.

2. Add the bread flour, and knead 4 to 6 minutes, adding additional bread flour if needed, until a smooth, elastic dough forms.

3. Cover the bowl with plastic wrap (but don't press the wrap directly onto the predough), and allow the predough to ferment until it has risen and is just starting to fall.

Main Dough

4. When the predough starts to fall, add the flour and sugar of the main dough to the predough in the bowl. With the mixer on low speed, add the extra virgin oil and the water. Then increase the mixer speed, and knead for 4 to 6 minutes, until the dough is smooth and elastic.

5. Divide the dough into 2 equal pieces, shape them loosely into balls, cover them so that they do not form a skin, and rest them on a floured surface for 30 minutes.

6. Coat 2 12-by-16-inch sheet pans liberally with the 2 tablespoons of olive oil. After the dough has rested, place each ball on a pan, and press the dough out with oiled hands until it will stretch no more.

7. Allow the dough to rise until it is as deep as the sheet pan, then press it out again, this time using only your fingertips, not only to spread the dough but also to dimple it.

Continued on page 114

8. Heat the oven to 480°F. Let the dough rise again until it is as deep as the sheet pan.

9. Spread 6 tablespoons of the herbed oil mixture very gently by hand over the proofed dough, and sprinkle with the sea salt.

10. Place the focaccia in the oven, and immediately reduce the heat to 350°F. Bake for 17 minutes, until the focaccia is a rich golden brown.

11. Remove the focaccia, place it on a work surface, and brush it with the remaining 4 tablespoons of herbed oil. Allow the focaccia to cool, then cut each pan into 8 rectangles. *

Herbed Oil

2 cups extra virgin olive oil

1 whole bulb garlic, roasted (recipe on page 00, step 4)

1¼ cups fresh herbs (rosemary plus sage, basil, and/or Italian parsley, if available)

1. In a medium saucepan, heat the oil until it is hot. Remove from the heat.

2. Cut the top off the garlic, and squeeze the soft cloves into the oil. Add the chopped herbs.

3. Let the herbs and garlic steep in and flavor the oil for at least 5 minutes. You may store the oil indefinitely in the refrigerator. (Yield: about 2½ cups.) *

Variation: Potato Focaccia

Thinly slice 2 medium red potatoes, and marinate them in the herbed oil while you prepare the dough. Drain the potatoes well before spreading 6 tablespoons of the oil on the focaccia. Then lay the potatoes, overlapping like fish scales, over the top of the focaccia. Bake as in the main recipe.

Variation: Kalamata Olive and Walnut Focaccia

Marinate ½ cups pitted Kalamata olives and ½ cup walnuts in the herbed oil while you prepare the dough. Drain them before spreading 6 tablespoons of the oil on the dough. Then scatter the olives and walnuts over the focaccia, and bake.

Pizza Dough

Greg Tompkins

The idea of pizza seems to have been borrowed from the Greeks and Etruscans. Historical documents detail the Romans' enjoyment of seasoned rounds of bread, and by A.D. 1000, *picea*, a disk of dough covered with herbs and spices, was common in Naples. The "modern" pizza is generally credited to Naples around 1830.

Tomatoes were not included until in the late 1600s, because the fruit was originally considered ornamental and poisonous. Cheese was added in the very late 1800s when an Italian baker topped a tomato and basil base with white mozzarella to mimic the colors of the Italian flag, in honor of Queen Margherita. To this day, the combination is known as Pizza Margherita.

6½ cups bread flour

2 tablespoons sugar

2 teaspoons salt

2 packages rapid-rise dry yeast

2 cups water

½ cup extra virgin olive oil

1. Combine all the dry ingredients, and stir to blend. In the bowl of a mixer fitted with a dough hook, knead the dry ingredients on low speed while you slowly pour in the liquid ingredients until a dough forms. Increase to medium speed, and knead for 6 to 8 minutes, until the dough is smooth and elastic.

2. Form the dough into a ball, and place it in a lightly oiled bowl, turning the dough to coat it with the oil. Cover the bowl with plastic wrap, and allow the dough to rise in a warm place until doubled, approximately 1 hour.

3. Punch the dough down, knead it briefly by hand, then reform it into a ball, and repeat step 2.

4. The dough will make either 2 16-inch pizzas, or 4 12-inch pizzas, or 4 10-inch calzones, or 10 8-inch pizzas or calzones, or 36 3-inch appetizer pizzettes or calzones.

5. Heat the oven to 500°F.

6. Place the shaped dough on a pizza pan, sheet pan, or pizza stone. Add the topping of your choice, and bake for 10 to 15 minutes. ✳

Variation: Cornmeal Pizza Dough

Replace 2 cups of the bread flour with 2 cups of yellow cornmeal.

Continued on page 116

Variation: Whole-Wheat Pizza Dough

Replace 3¼ cups of the bread flour with 3¼ cups of whole-wheat flour. Replace the sugar with 2 tablespoons of honey. Combine the honey with the liquid ingredients instead of the dry ingredients.

Variation: New York Pizza Dough

Omit the sugar and oil, and increase the water to 2¼ cups.

Variation: Sweet Pizza Dough

Increase the sugar to ¼ cup, and (optional) substitute a flavorless vegetable oil for the olive oil.

Desserts

✷

Champagne-Chocolate-Chestnut Torte

Teresa Douglas/Mitchell

This rich cake has an unusual component, chestnut puree, which provides an interesting taste and a long shelf life.

Other nut butters, such as peanut and cashew, are wonderful variations. A garnish of shaved chocolate curls can elevate the simple elegance of the cake to something quite spectacular.

Serves 16

1 pound fine quality semisweet chocolate, chopped

½ cup champagne

4 ounces butter, softened

1⅝ cups heavy cream

1 pound unsweetened chestnut puree

1½ cups granulated sugar

½ cup flour

Pinch of salt

6 eggs

About ¼ cup plus 2 tablespoons confectioners' sugar

1. Heat the oven to 350°F. Butter a 10-inch springform pan, and line the bottom with parchment paper.

2. Melt the chocolate with the champagne in a double boiler. Remove from the heat, and cool.

3. In a large electric mixer bowl, blend the butter, ⅝ cup of the cream, and the chestnut puree until smooth. Beat in the chocolate mixture and then the granulated sugar.

4. Add the flour and salt. Beat in the eggs, one at a time.

5. Pour the batter into the springform pan.

6. Bake for 1 hour, 10 minutes, until set.

7. Cool on a rack before removing from the pan. Dust the cooled cake with 2 tablespoons of the confectioners' sugar.

8. Whip the remaining 1 cup of cream with the remaining ¼ cup of confectioners' sugar (or less or more to your taste) to make Chantilly cream.

9. Transfer the Chantilly cream to a pastry bag, and pipe it in rosettes around the cake. *

Persimmon-Walnut Cake

Teresa Douglas / Mitchell

⋇

I particularly like the eclectic flavor combination of the persimmon, ginger,
and cinnamon with the chocolate and walnuts in this cake.

Serves 12

1½ cups coarsely chopped walnuts

1½ cups bittersweet chocolate chunks or chips

3 cups flour

1 tablespoon baking powder

1 teaspoon ground cinnamon

1 teaspoon ground ginger
(or 1 tablespoon minced candied ginger)

½ teaspoon freshly grated nutmeg

1 cup (2 sticks) unsalted butter, softened

2 cups sugar

1½ cups persimmon (or pumpkin) puree

4 eggs

¾ cup champagne (or buttermilk)

1. Heat the oven to 325°F.

2. In a medium bowl, toss the walnuts and chocolate with ½ cup of the flour. Set aside.

3. Sift the remaining flour with the baking powder, cinnamon, ginger, and nutmeg into a medium bowl. Set aside.

4. In a large mixer bowl, cream the butter and sugar for 8 minutes, until fluffy. Beat in the persimmon puree, and then the eggs, one at a time.

5. Fold in the flour mixture in thirds alternately with the champagne. Stir in the walnut mixture.

6. Pour the batter into an ungreased 10-inch tube or Bundt pan.

7. Bake for 1 hour, 15 minutes. Cool on a rack for 45 minutes, and remove from the pan. ⋇

Chocolate Ganache Cake

Bo Friberg

This cake makes a wonderful dessert for a special occasion. Its appearance is very impressive, the entire cake can be completed several days in advance, and everyone loves the rich chocolate filling, flavored with honey and hazelnut liqueur. For a less challenging presentation, omit the ribbon sponge on the sides of the cake and/or simply top each serving with a rosette of whipped cream and chocolate shavings (made using a melon baller or vegetable peeler) instead of making the cookie butterflies.

Serves 24

Ganache Filling

1 pound, 12 ounces dark sweet chocolate

6 ounces unsweetened chocolate

5 cups heavy cream

8 egg yolks

1/3 cup sugar

1/2 cup honey

1/3 cup Frangelico liqueur
(hazelnut-flavored liqueur)

Cake

1 15-by-22-inch Ribbon Sponge Sheet Cake
(recipe on page 122)

2 10-inch circles thin chocolate sponge cake
(your favorite recipe or purchased)

3 tablespoons unsweetened cocoa powder

24 Cookie Butterflies (recipe on page 124)

24 edible flowers

Ganache Filling

1. Chop the sweet and unsweetened chocolates into small chunks. Place them all in a bowl set over simmering water, and melt. Set aside, but keep warm.

2. Whip the cream until it forms soft peaks. Set aside in the refrigerator.

3. In a large mixer bowl, whip the egg yolks with the sugar for about 2 minutes, until the mixture is light yellow and fluffy.

4. Bring the honey to a boil. With the mixer running at medium speed, gradually pour the honey into the egg yolk mixture. Turn to high speed, and continue whipping until the mixture is cold.

5. Fold in the warm chocolate and the Frangelico liqueur. Quickly stir in the whipped cream.

6. Set aside while you prepare the cake. (If you are not proceeding within an hour, refrigerate the filling. Before using, place the bowl over barely simmering water, and stir with a spoon until smooth. Do not overheat, or you will melt and deflate the filling.)

Cake

7. Cut 1¾-inch strips, crosswise, from the ribbon sponge.

8. Place 2 10-inch cake rings on 12-inch cardboard circles for support. Line the inside of the rings with strips of parchment paper or acetate (thick plastic).

Continued on page 122

9. Place the ribbon sponge strips inside the parchment inside the rings so that the striped side of the cake is facing the ring. The ribbons will be vertical on the cakes.

10. Place a chocolate sponge circle in the bottom of each ring. Adjust the rings, if necessary, to fit snugly against the sponge circles.

11. Divide the ganache filling between the 2 cake rings. Smooth the tops carefully to make them even, because the cakes will not be iced, simply dusted with cocoa. Cover the cakes, without touching the filling, and chill them in the refrigerator for at least 2 hours to set the filling.

12. When you are ready to serve, remove the cake rings and parchment strips. Sift 1 tablespoon of the cocoa powder lightly over the tops of the cakes.

13. Using a knife dipped in hot water, cut the cakes into 12 servings each. Wipe the knife, and dip it into hot water after each cut. Place a cookie butterfly on top of each slice at the outside edge, pressing the cookie into the cake gently so it sticks.

14. Sift the remaining cocoa powder lightly over the base of 24 dessert plates. Place a slice of cake in the center of each plate. Place an edible flower on the cocoa next to each slice. ✳

Ribbon Sponge Sheet Cake

2 cups Chocolate Tulip Paste (recipe on page 197)

5 eggs

1 scant cup sugar

2 cups finely ground, blanched almonds (almond meal), not packed

2 tablespoons bread flour

1/2 cup egg whites

4 tablespoons unsalted butter, melted

4 ounces (or less—see step 13) cocoa butter, melted

This is a fairly complicated technique that requires tools most nonprofessionals do not have. You can prepare the Chocolate Ganache Cake without the ribbon sponge on the sides. Just skip steps 7 and 9 on page 120 and above, this page.

This recipe makes 2 sponge sheets; you need only 1 for the ganache cake.

1. On each of 2 silicon mats, spread half of the Chocolate Tulip Paste into a rectangle 22 by 15 inches and about 1/16 inch thick. Using a trowel with square notches spaced 1/8 inch apart, remove half of the paste in straight lines, lengthwise. To keep the lines straight, place a piece of wood (or any suitable object) about 1 inch high at each short end of the silicon mat. Position a long ruler across, resting on the wood supports, and guide the scraper across, leaning against the ruler.

2. Place the silicon mats on top of inverted sheet pans, and place them in the refrigerator for at laest 30 minutes (or in the freezer for 10 minutes) to firm the tulip paste while you make the ribbon sponge base.

3. Place the whole eggs and about ½ cup of the sugar in a medium mixer bowl set over simmering water. Heat the mixture to 120°F, stirring constantly. Remove from the heat, and whip at high speed for 1 minute.

4. In a small bowl, thoroughly combine the ground almonds and flour. Set aside.

5. In a large bowl, whip the egg whites with the remaining sugar until just before soft peaks form.

6. Carefully fold the almond mixture into the whole egg mixture.

7. Gently fold the melted butter into the whole egg mixture.

8. Gradually fold the whole egg mixture into the egg white mixture.

9. Heat the oven to 550°F. Set 2 large sheets of parchment paper on a work surface.

10. Take out the chilled tulip paste strips, but leave the mats in place on the sheet pans. Divide the ribbon sponge base batter between the 2 silicon mats, and spread it evenly on top of the chocolate lines. Tap the pans quite firmly against the table to set the batter and remove air bubbles.

11. Bake immediately for about 4 minutes, until the sponge begins to color slightly.

12. Remove the sponge sheets from the oven, and dust the tops lightly with flour. Invert the sheets onto the parchment paper, and let cool for 2 minutes. Carefully peel away the silicon mats.

13. Spray (or brush) the melted cocoa butter over the sheets, to help keep the sheets flexible and prevent them from sticking to the forms or rings when used in desserts. (You'll need less melted cocoa butter if you brush it on; the 4 ounces are needed for a spray bottle to work well.)

14. Cover the ribbon sponge sheets with plastic wrap, and store them in the refrigerator or freezer until needed. (Yield: 2 22-by-15-inch sheets.) *

Continued on page 124

Cookie Butterflies

4 cups Vanilla Tulip Paste (recipe on page 197)

1 teaspoon unsweetened cocoa powder

1. Make a butterfly-shaped stencil using 1/16-inch-thick cardboard. Cut a 6-by-16-inch rectangle out of corrugated cardboard, and score it across the center so that you can fold it in half on the long edge, to make a V. Tape across the top edges to secure the shape, but leave the top of the V open.

2. Heat the oven to 425°F. Grease and flour the backs of 4 clean, even sheet pans (or use silicon mats, which do not need to be greased and floured). Tap the pans to remove excess flour.

3. Color 2 tablespoons of the tulip paste with the cocoa powder. Place a little of the cocoa-colored paste in a piping bag, and refill the bag as needed.

4. Place the butterfly stencil on a sheet pan. Spread the plain tulip paste inside the stencil, lift the stencil, and place it on the next area of the pan. Repeat, making at least 24 flat and even butterfly shapes on the 4 sheet pans.

5. Pipe small decorative dots of the cocoa-colored paste on the wings of the butterflies.

6. Bake one pan at a time for about 4 minutes, until a few light brown spots appear on the cookies. While the cookies are baking, invert a muffin tin, and place the V-shaped cardboard between two muffin cups.

7. Leave the pan in the oven, and remove the cookie butterfly that is most done. Working quickly, set the butterfly cookie inside the cardboard V, and press gently, so that the wings are shaped at a 45° angle. Set the cookie aside until firm. Repeat to form the remaining butterflies.

8. Repeat steps 6 and 7 with the other pans.

9. Store the cookies in an airtight container at room temperature until needed. They will keep for several days. *

Cornmeal Pound Cake

Linda Carucci

✳

Serve this cake with Fresh and Dried Fruit Compote (recipe on page 126).
For best results, have all the ingredients at room temperature.

Serves 14

1 cup flour

¼ teaspoon salt

⅛ teaspoon baking powder

¾ cup (1½ sticks) unsalted butter

1¼ cups sugar

3 large eggs

1 teaspoon vanilla

1 teaspoon finely grated lemon zest

½ cup yellow cornmeal

1. Adjust the oven rack to the lower third of the oven. Heat the oven to 350°F. Generously butter a 10-by-4-inch ribbed deer-back pan, or a 4- to 5-cup (9-by-5-by-3-inch) loaf pan, or a 6-cup ring mold about 9½ inches in diameter. Dust the pan with cornmeal, and tap out the excess.

2. Sift the flour, salt, and baking powder into a small bowl. Set aside.

3. In the large bowl of an electric mixer fitted with a paddle, cream the butter at medium speed, until creamy and smooth. Add the sugar, and beat until fluffy. Add the eggs, one at a time, beating well after each addition. Add the vanilla and lemon zest.

4. Add the flour mixture to the butter mixture. Stir in the cornmeal until well blended.

5. Spread the batter evenly in the prepared pan. Bake for about 60 minutes, until a wooden toothpick inserted in the center of the cake comes out free of batter.

6. Remove the cake from the oven, and cool it in the pan for about 10 minutes. Invert the cake onto a wire rack, and lift off the cake pan. Cool the cake completely, cut into thin slices, and serve. ✳

Fresh and Dried Fruit Compote

Linda Carucci

✳

Serve this chunky fruit sauce with Cornmeal Pound Cake (recipe on page 125) or over vanilla ice cream.

Serves 8

3 cups white wine,
preferably a fruity one such as chenin blanc

3 tablespoons sugar

1 teaspoon finely grated orange zest

$1/3$ cup each golden raisins, dried
cranberries, and dried sweet cherries

5 small (5-ounce) navel oranges,
peeled and sectioned

2 small bananas, quartered lengthwise
and cut crosswise into $1/2$-inch pieces

1 cup fresh strawberries, cleaned,
hulled, and quartered

1 large (10-ounce) pomegranate
to yield about $1 1/4$ cups pomegranate seeds

1. In a medium saucepan, heat the wine, sugar, and orange zest just to a boil. Remove from the heat, and add the raisins, cranberries, and cherries. Set aside until cool.

2. When cool, pour into a serving dish. Add the orange sections, banana slices, and strawberries, and mix gently. Sprinkle the pomegranate seeds over the compote. ✳

Pâte Brisée

Michael Kalanty

✳

Whether you use its French or American name (flaky pie dough), stock your freezer with this
staple of the pastry kitchen to streamline your dessert making. It will keep, frozen, for up to 2 months.
Thaw it in the refrigerator before using.

1¼ cups all-purpose flour

⅛ teaspoon salt

2 teaspoons sugar

4 ounces unsalted butter, chilled

2 to 6 teaspoons ice water

1. Combine the flour, salt, and sugar on a work surface.

2. Cut the butter into the dry ingredients, using a pastry cutter or large fork, until the mixture resembles coarse meal. Transfer the mixture to a medium stainless steel bowl.

3. Gradually add the ice water, tossing the mixture with a fork until the dough just comes together.

4. Gather the dough into a ball, wrap it in plastic, and flatten it into a disk about 1 inch thick. Refrigerate for at least 20 minutes.

5. Roll the dough out as directed in recipes calling for flaky dough. (Yield: 1 9-inch pie crust.) ✳

Pear Frangipane Galette

Michael Kalanty

The classic combination of pears and almond is highlighted in this free-form "tart" baked without the traditional tart pan.

Serves 6

1 recipe *pâte brisée*, chilled
(recipe on page 127)

1 ounce almond paste at room temperature

5 tablespoons plus 2 teaspoons sugar

1 large egg yolk

2 tablespoons unsalted butter

2 teaspoons milk

1/4 teaspoon vanilla

1 teaspoon fresh lemon juice

Pinch salt

1/2 cup all-purpose flour

5 underripe pears (Bosc or Bartlett),
peeled, halved, and cored

1/3 cup apricot preserves (or jam)

2 teaspoons water

1. On a lightly floured surface, roll the *pâte brisée* into a circle 1/4 inch thick. Dock it all over with a fork. Transfer it to a baking tray lined with parchment paper, and refrigerate for 20 to 30 minutes.

2. Meanwhile, prepare the frangipane: In a medium bowl, cream the almond paste with 1 tablespoon of the sugar. Add the egg yolk, and beat until creamy. Add the butter and 2 tablespoons of the remaining sugar, and beat for 1 minute. Scrape down the sides of the bowl. Add the milk, vanilla, lemon juice, and salt, and beat to incorporate fully. Add the flour in thirds, beating for 20 seconds after each addition. Cover, and refrigerate until needed.

3. Cut the *pâte brisée* into an 11-inch circle. Brush the edge of the dough with water, and fold over a 3/4-inch border. Press down with a fork to seal the edges and form a rim. Refrigerate for 10 minutes.

4. Adjust the oven rack to the middle of the oven. Heat the oven to 400°F.

5. Spread the prepared frangipane over the pastry shell.

6. Place the pears on a cutting board, cut side down, and slice them lengthwise 1/8 inch thick. Keep the slices of each half together. Sprinkle the pears with the 2 teaspoons of sugar to prevent browning.

7. With both hands, transfer a sliced pear half to the outer edge of the pastry shell, setting it just inside the rim. Press down to fan out the slices.

8. Continue arranging the slices in this manner to fill the pastry shell with overlapping concentric rings.

Continued on page 130

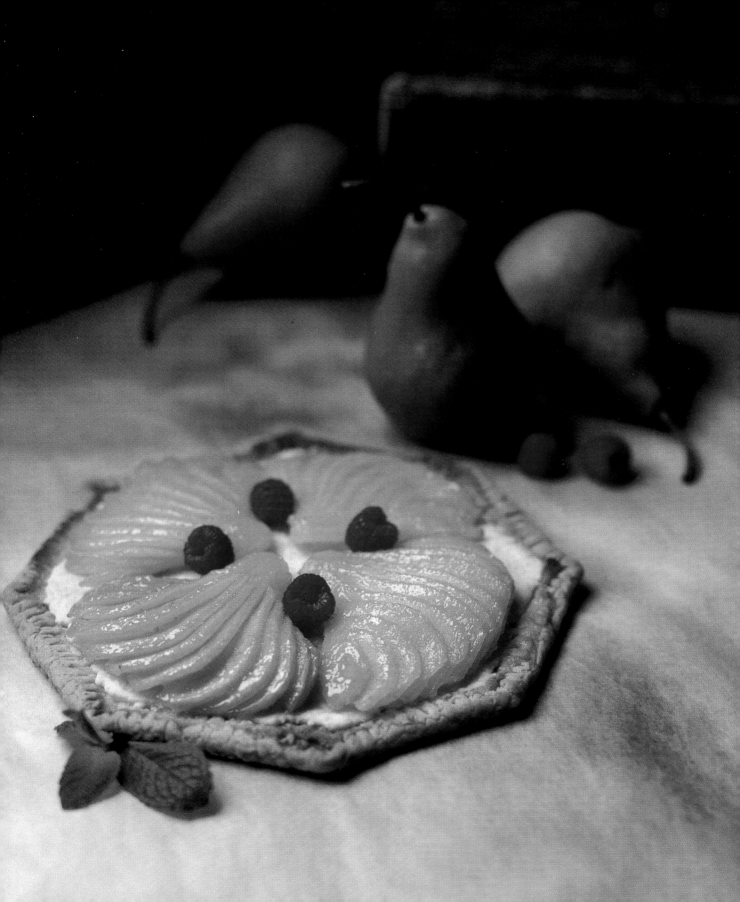

9. Sprinkle the remaining 2 tablespoons of sugar over the pears.

10. Place the galette in the oven, and immediately reduce the temperature to 375°F. Bake for 45 to 55 minutes, until the pears are soft, the crust is golden, and the frangipane has risen and set in the center of the galette. (The edges of the pears will begin to brown. If they start to get too brown before the filling is set, gently cover the edges of the galette with parchment paper.)

11. Remove the galette from the oven, and cool it on a rack for 30 minutes.

12. While the galette cools, heat the apricot preserves with the water in a small saucepan over low heat. Press the mixture through a fine strainer. Return the strained apricot to the stove to reheat.

13. When the galette has cooled for 30 minutes, brush the pears with a thin layer of apricot. Allow it to cool for 5 minutes. Transfer the galette to a serving platter.

14. If desired, you may also glaze the edges of the fruit as follows: Adjust the broiler rack to 4 inches from the heat source, and heat the broiler. Cut a 2-inch ring of aluminum foil to lay over the outer edge of the galette. Place the glazed galette under the broiler for 1 to 2 minutes, until the edges of the pears are nicely browned. Remove the foil before serving. ✳

Apple Pie with Crème Fraîche and Black Pepper

Michael Kalanty

✳

The subtle addition of freshly cracked black pepper lends a hint of spiciness to
this luscious two-crust pie, inspired by the flavors of Brittany, France.

Serves 8

2 recipes *pâte brisée*, chilled
(recipe on page 127)

2½ pounds baking apples (Granny Smith,
Stayman Winesap, etc.), peeled and cored

About ¾ cup plus 1 teaspoon sugar

2 tablespoons fresh lime juice

Pinch salt

¼ teaspoon freshly cracked black pepper

4 tablespoons flour

¼ cup Calvados (or apple brandy)

½ cup crème fraîche
(recipe on page 196) (or sour cream)

About 1 tablespoon milk

1. Adjust the oven rack to the middle of the oven. Heat the oven to 425°F.

2. On a lightly floured surface, roll out the 2 *pâtes brisées* to circles ⅛ inch thick. Line a 9-inch pie pan with 1 circle. Trim the excess, leaving a 1-inch overhang of dough. Refrigerate the pan and the second dough circle for at least 20 minutes.

3. Cut the apples into ¼-inch slices. Place them in a large stainless steel bowl with the ¾ cup of sugar, lime juice, salt, pepper, and flour. Toss to coat the apples evenly. Add the Calvados and crème fraîche. Toss to mix well.

4. Allow the mixture to sit at room temperature, covered, for 20 minutes. Taste the mixture, and add sugar if necessary.

5. Transfer the apple mixture to the prepared pie pan. Brush the edge of the dough with some of the milk, and place the second *pâte brisée* circle over the top. Press to seal the edges. Trim off the excess dough, leaving a 1-inch overhang.

6. Roll the edge of the dough under, forming a ridge around the edge of the pie pan. Decoratively crimp the edge of the dough.

7. Brush the top with the remaining milk, and sprinkle it with the remaining teaspoon of sugar. Cut three small vents in the dough with a paring knife. Place the pie on a baking tray and then in the oven. Bake for 15 minutes, reduce the heat to 375°F, and bake for about 55 minutes more, until the crust is crisp and the apples are tender when pierced with a knife inserted through a vent in the crust. Remove from the oven, and cool on a rack for 30 minutes. ✳

Chilled Mochaccino Pie

Michael Kalanty

✴

A dessert or a rich coffee drink? Serve this chocolate-espresso custard pie guaranteed to satisfy either craving.

Serves 8

1 recipe *pâte brisée*, chilled
(recipe on page 127)

2 teaspoons powdered gelatin

6 ounces strong espresso

8 large eggs, separated

¾ cup plus 10 tablespoons sugar

4 ounces semisweet chocolate,
melted and kept warm

¼ teaspoon cream of tartar

1½ cups heavy cream

1 teaspoon vanilla extract

1½ teaspoons ground cinnamon

1. Heat the oven to 375°F.

2. On a lightly floured surface, roll the *pâte brisée* out to a circle ⅛ inch thick. Line a 9-inch pie pan with the dough. Trim the excess, leaving a ½-inch overhang of dough.

3. Roll up the edge of the dough to form a rim, and decoratively crimp the edges. Dock the dough all over with a fork. Refrigerate for 30 minutes.

4. Place a 12-inch circle of parchment paper over the dough, and fill the shell with pie weights (or uncooked rice or beans, to be discarded afterward). Bake the pie shell for 20 minutes.

5. Remove the weights and parchment paper. Return the shell to the oven, and bake for 12 to 15 minutes more, until golden brown. Remove from the oven, and cool on a rack to room temperature.

6. Meanwhile, sprinkle the gelatin over the espresso in a small bowl. Allow 15 minutes for the gelatin to absorb the liquid.

7. Combine the egg yolks and ¾ cup plus 2 tablespoons of the sugar in a medium stainless steel bowl. Whisk for about 2 minutes, until lightly frothy.

8. Place the espresso mixture over a bain-marie with barely simmering water. When it is liquefied, pour it into the egg yolk mixture. Then place the yolk mixture over barely simmering water, and whisk for about 10 minutes, until it is thick. Remove from the heat, and allow to cool, whisking occasionally.

9. Pour a third of the espresso mixture into the melted chocolate, and mix well. Fold the chocolate mixture back into the remaining espresso mixture, half at a time. Refrigerate for 30 minutes.

10. In a stainless steel bowl, whisk the egg whites and cream of tartar to soft peaks. Add 4 tablespoons of the remaining sugar, and beat until firm peaks form.

11. Fold the egg white mixture into the cooled espresso mixture by thirds.

12. Spoon the mixture into the cooled baked pie shell. Refrigerate for at least 2 hours, until the filling is firm.

13. Whip the cream with the remaining 4 tablespoons of sugar and the vanilla until firm peaks form.

14. Fit a pastry bag with a star tip, and fill the bag with the whipped cream mixture. Decorate the top of the pie with the cream, and dust with the cinnamon. *

Pasticiotti

Linda Carucci

These double-crusted Italian tartlets are filled with sweetened ricotta. Alternatively, you may fill them with rum-spiked vanilla or chocolate custard. They may be served chilled or at room temperature. I prefer them chilled.

Serves 12

Filling

2 cups (1 pound) whole-milk ricotta

2 tablespoons flour

2 tablespoons sugar

2 eggs, lightly beaten

1/4 cup semisweet or bittersweet chocolate chips (optional)

1 teaspoon vanilla extract

1 tablespoon rum (optional)

Crust

1 1/2 cups shortening

2 cups sugar

4 eggs

2 teaspoons honey

4 cups flour

2 teaspoons baking powder

1 tablespoon water

Confectioners' sugar for decoration

Filling

1. Place the ricotta in a medium-mesh strainer, and let excess liquid drain off.

2. Transfer the ricotta to a medium bowl. Add the flour and sugar, and mix to combine.

3. Add the eggs, and mix. Stir in the chocolate chips, vanilla, and rum. Refrigerate until ready to use.

Crust

4. In a mixer with a paddle attachment, cream together the shortening and sugar.

5. Add 3 of the eggs, one at a time, mixing well after each addition.

6. Add the honey, and mix well.

7. In a large bowl, stir together the flour and baking powder. Add to the mixer bowl, and mix just until the dough comes together.

8. Cover the bowl with plastic wrap, and chill the dough in the refrigerator for 1 to 24 hours.

9. Remove the dough from the refrigerator, and let it stand at room temperature for 30 minutes. Divide it into thirds. Put one-third aside in a cool place.

10. Assemble 12 3½-inch tartlet pans with removable bottoms. Pat two-thirds of the dough into the bottoms and sides of the pans.

11. Heat the oven to 350°F.

12. Fill each dough-lined tartlet pan three-fourths full with the ricotta filling.

13. Using a rolling pin or the heel of your hand, shape 12 top crusts for the tartlets from the reserved dough. Using a metal scraper, carefully transfer the top crusts onto the tartlets. Seal the edges by pressing with your fingers. Place the *pasticiotti* on a sheet pan.

14. Beat the remaining egg with the water to make an egg wash. Brush a light coating of the wash on each top crust. Bake the tartlets for 25 to 35 minutes, until the top crusts are golden brown. (To achieve even browning, you may have to rotate the sheet pan after 20 minutes.)

15. Transfer the tartlets to a wire rack, and let them cool for 15 minutes. Then carefully remove the *pasticiotti* from the tartlet pans, and set them on the wire rack to cool completely.

16. Sprinkle the *pasticiotti* with sifted confectioners' sugar, and serve immediately. (Alternatively, chill the cooled *pasticiotti* in the refrigerator for 2 hours before sprinkling with confectioners' sugar.) Store any leftover *pasticiotti* in the refrigerator. ✻

Raspberry Tea Tarts

Teresa Douglas / Mitchell

This recipe uses low-fat ingredients to make it more heart-healthy. If you prefer
a more decadent dessert, use regular butter and cream cheese.

Before you use your tartlet molds the first time, it is a good idea to season them with
oil and bake them for an hour or so in a low oven. This should alleviate sticking, especially if you
simply wipe the molds out to clean them after use.

Serves 24

Crust

6 ounces low-fat cream cheese

1 cup (2 sticks) margarine

2 cups flour

2 tablespoons granulated sugar

1/4 teaspoon salt

Filling

16 ounces low-fat cream cheese

1/2 cup plus 4 tablespoons confectioners' sugar

4 cups fresh (or frozen) raspberries

1. Heat the oven to 375°F.

2. Blend the 6 ounces of cream cheese and the margarine together in a food processor until smooth.

3. Add the flour, granulated sugar, and salt, and pulse until the dough forms a ball. Chill for 45 minutes.

4. Meanwhile, whip the 16 ounces of cream cheese with the 1/2 cup of confectioners' sugar. Set aside.

5. Roll the crust dough out on a floured work surface. Cut the dough into circles a little larger than the diameter of your tartlet molds. Chill the circles again for 20 minutes.

6. Press the circles into the tartlet molds, and prick the dough with a fork.

7. Bake the tart shells for 12 to 14 minutes, until they are lightly browned.

8. Fill each tart shell with a dollop of the cream cheese filling, and cover the top with raspberries. Dust the tarts with the 4 tablespoons of confectioners' sugar. (Yield: 24 2 1/2-inch tarts.) *

Variation: Lemon Curd Tea Tarts

Omit the cream cheese, confectioners' sugar, and raspberries, and fill the tarts with lemon curd from the recipe for Lemon Curd Parfait on page 137.

Lemon Curd Parfait

Teresa Douglas / Mitchell

⁎

Lemon curd is a distinctive British dish and a nice foil to some of the sweeter foods associated with tea.
It is quite versatile: spoon it into tartlet shells, layer it with cakes, or combine it with Chantilly cream for an airy mousse.

Serves 8

Lemon Curd

6 teaspoons grated lemon zest

5/8 cup lemon juice

1 cup (2 sticks) butter

2 cups sugar

8 eggs, beaten

Chantilly Cream

4 cups heavy cream, whipped

About 4 tablespoons sugar

8 sprigs mint

Lemon Curd

1. Place the zest, lemon juice, butter, and sugar in the top of a double boiler. Stir over simmering water for 10 minutes, until the butter is melted and the sugar is dissolved.

2. Temper the eggs by stirring a small amount of the hot lemon mixture into them. Then add them to the lemon mixture. Stir constantly over the hot water for about 20 minutes, until thickened. Chill thoroughly. (The lemon curd will keep for up to 2 weeks refrigerated.)

Chantilly Cream

3. Whip the cream with enough of the sugar to sweeten it to your taste.

4. Alternate spoonfuls of lemon curd and Chantilly cream in 8 stemmed dessert glasses. Garnish with the mint. ⁎

Crème Caramel Nouvelle

Bo Friberg

Correct preparation of an individual baked custard is a technique included in any comprehensive pastry course. While classic *crème caramel* has been a standard offering on restaurant menus for years, the original version can be a little boring. This recipe, with ginger flavoring and a dressed up presentation, is a good example of how easy it can be to make a ho-hum dessert exciting with a little attention and imagination.

Serves 16

Gingered Caramel Custard

2 tablespoons finely chopped fresh ginger

2 quarts milk

5 cups sugar

4 drops lemon juice

1/2 cup water

16 eggs

Garnishes

2 pounds assorted fresh seasonal fruit
(3 or 4 kinds with contrasting colors, if possible)

1/4 cup orange liqueur

1 1/4 cups Caramel Sauce
(recipe on page 140)

16 Pirouette Cookies
(recipe on page 140)

16 Caramel Spirals
(recipe on page 141)

Gingered Caramel Custard

1. Heat the oven to 350°F.

2. Combine the ginger and milk in a large saucepan, and bring to the scalding point. Set aside off the heat to infuse.

3. Place 3 cups of the sugar in a heavy medium saucepan. Add the lemon juice and water, and stir. Cook over low heat, without stirring, until caramelized to a dark, golden brown color.

4. Pour a 1/8-inch layer of caramel on the bottoms of 16 3-inch-diameter soufflé ramekins (or coffee cups with straight sides). Set the ramekins aside.

5. Reheat the milk mixture to the scalding point. In a large bowl, whisk together the remaining 2 cups of sugar and the eggs. Gradually add the hot milk mixture, whisking constantly. Strain the custard, and discard the ginger.

6. Pour the custard into the ramekins. Place them in a large baking pan, and add hot water around them until it reaches up the sides of the ramekins to just below the level of the custard.

7. Bake for about 35 minutes, until the custard is set. Let cool completely, then refrigerate until ready to serve. The custard can be stored this way for several days.

Garnishes

8. Cut the fruit into pieces about the size of a raspberry, keeping each variety separate until serving time.

Continued on page 140

9. When you are ready to serve, combine the fruit and the orange liqueur gently, so that you do not bruise the fruit. If you are using a red fruit that tends to "bleed," leave it out, and add it to the plates last.

10. Unmold the custards, and place one in the center of each dessert plate. Use a plastic squeeze bottle to pipe just enough Caramel Sauce around the custard to cover the base of the plate.

11. Arrange some of the prepared fruit on top of the sauce, using 2 or 3 pieces of each variety.

12. Gently push a Pirouette Cookie into the center of each custard. Make sure it is standing straight.

13. Place a Caramel Spiral on top of each cookie, and let the spiral fall around the custard. Serve immediately. ✳

Caramel Sauce

2⅓ cups sugar

1 teaspoon lemon juice

1⅓ cups water

1. In a heavy, large saucepan, mix the sugar and lemon juice. Cook over low heat, stirring, until the sugar has caramelized to a golden brown. Remove the pan from the heat, and carefully pour in the water. (The mixture will sputter.) Return the pan to the heat, and cook, stirring constantly, to dissolve any lumps.

2. Let the sauce cool completely. Add water if needed to thin to a saucelike consistency. Be sure to wait until the sauce has cooled completely before judging its thickness. The sauce may be covered and stored in the refrigerator for up to 2 weeks. (Yield: about 1½ cups.) ✳

Pirouette Cookies

1 teaspoon unsweetened cocoa powder

4 cups Vanilla Tulip Paste (recipe on page 197)

1. Heat the oven to 425°F. Grease and flour the backs of 4 clean, even sheet pans (or use silicon mats, which do not need to be greased and floured). Make a 3¾-by-4½-inch rectangular stencil out of ¹⁄₁₆-inch-thick cardboard.

2. Mix the cocoa powder into 2 tablespoons of the tulip paste, and place a portion of the cocoa-colored paste in a small piping bag. (Refill the bag as needed.)

3. Place the stencil on one of the sheet pans, and spread a thin layer of tulip paste evenly inside it. Lift the stencil, and set it on another area of the pan. Repeat to make 16 rectangles, with no more than 4 per pan.

4. Cut a small opening in the piping bag, and pipe 3 straight lines of cocoa-colored tulip paste, close to each other, diagonally across the center of each rectangle.

5. Bake one pan at a time for 4 to 5 minutes, until the tulip paste is dry and the first cookie is beginning to show brown spots.

6. Remove the cookie that is most done, and quickly wrap the 4½-inch edges around a 1-inch dowel. Press the cookie for 3 to 5 seconds to shape it, then slide it off the dowel and set it aside.

7. Repeat steps 5–6 until all the cookies are shaped.

8. Store the cookies in an airtight container in a warm dry place. They will keep for up to 3 weeks. (Yield: 16 cookies.) *

Caramel Spirals

3 cups sugar

¾ cup water

1 tablespoon light corn syrup

Working with caramelized sugar, it is easy to get burned unless you are very careful. Keep a bowl of ice water handy to your work area, and if you do have a mishap immerse the burned part into the water for a minute or more, to alleviate the injury.

1. Place the sugar and water in a copper pan; stir to combine.

2. Bring to a boil, boil for 1 minute, then add the corn syrup. Lower the heat to medium so that the mixture will not boil too hard, and cook without stirring. Instead, brush down the sides of the pan with water every 3 to 4 minutes, until the sugar reaches the hard ball stage, about 260°F. Keep boiling, but without brushing down, until the sugar has caramelized to a dark golden brown (about 320°F).

3. Quickly remove the pan from the heat, and place the bottom of the pan in cold water to stop the cooking process. Let the caramel cool until it is the consistency of a thick syrup.

4. Using a double thickness of parchment, make a few disposable pastry bags. The thickness will prevent the bags from breaking as you pipe, which can cause serious burns, and also helps to protect your hands from the heat as you are working. Fold the bottom 2 inches of the tip back against one side, making a sharp crease at the fold, to seal the bottom while you fill the bag with caramel.

5. Set out 3 silicon mats (or thick sheets of reusable silicon-coated parchment paper; the thinner type tends to buckle).

Continued on page 142

6. When the caramel is cool enough to pipe the spirals, carefully pour about 1 cup into a pastry bag. Do not attempt to work with more than this at once. (If the caramel is too hot to pipe, it will shrink into little droplets instead of forming a line when it hits the cooler surface. Allow it to cool more.) Wrap a towel around the bag, cut a small opening in the tip, and unfold the 2 inches of tip, so that the caramel can reach the opening.

7. Pipe out spirals about 7 inches in diameter, starting in the center with a small teardrop, which will help balance the spiral on top of a dessert. You may close the spiral by piping the very last inch or so on top of the previous circle. Position the spirals so you can fit 6 on each silicon mat. The thinner the lines and the more concentric circles in each spiral, the more elegant the finished decorations; however, very thin spirals will break when you lift them off the mat, while very thick ones not only look clumsy but also will not flex and fall around the dessert. Even if the spiral is thin, if its circumference is not wide enough the outer rings won't have enough weight to pull the spiral down.

8. The spirals will set in 2 to 3 minutes. Keep them in a dry place until ready to use; humidity can damage them. Even under optimal conditions, they must be used within 2 hours after preparation. ✳

Basic Crepes

Michael Kalanty

✳

Make a batch of these and freeze them. They're an easy way to pull together any number of fancy recipes at the last minute; even leftovers become a special dish when wrapped in crepes!

1½ cups all-purpose flour

2 tablespoons sugar

¼ teaspoon salt

2 large eggs

2 large egg yolks

1 cup milk

1 cup water

2 tablespoons clarified butter

About 2 tablespoons butter

1. In a medium bowl, blend together the flour, sugar, and salt.

2. In a small bowl, combine the eggs, yolks, milk, and water. Gradually pour the egg mixture into the dry ingredients, and blend with a whisk until smooth. Cover, and let the batter stand at room temperature for 30 minutes.

3. Strain the batter, and add the clarified butter. The batter should be the consistency of light cream. Add cold water to thin it or up to 2 tablespoons of flour to thicken it, if necessary.

4. Melt ½ teaspoon of the butter in a 6-inch crepe pan over medium heat. Swirl the pan to coat the sides and bottom evenly. Pour 2 to 3 tablespoons of batter into the pan all at once, and swirl the pan quickly to spread the batter over the bottom of the pan.

5. Cook until the bottom of the crepe is golden brown, 1½ to 2 minutes. Toss the crepe or turn it with a spatula, and cook the other side about 30 seconds. Turn the crepe onto a plate.

6. Repeat with the remaining batter, melting more butter in the pan, as needed, to prevent sticking. Stack the crepes browned side up on top of one another as they are made. When cool, they can be frozen for up to 1 month, wrapped in stacks of 10 to 12 in heavy plastic. Frozen crepes may then be removed as needed. Thaw them completely before using. (Yield: about 24 6-inch crepes.) ✳

Variation: Buckwheat Crepes

Substitute ¾ cup buckwheat flour for ¾ cup of the all-purpose flour. Eliminate the eggs and egg yolks. Increase the milk to 1½ cups.

Crêpes à la Bretagne

Michael Kalanty

✷

Originating from the Brittany region of northwest France, these are a heartier version of the wheat flour crepe, made with buckwheat flour and no eggs. Since they use the whole grain, they lend an earthy, rustic note to any dish in which they are used. One of the many ways the Bretons favor them is heated through and spread with sweet jams. Serve them as a dessert or part of an afternoon tea. Filled with boysenberry or pear preserves, they make an interesting accompaniment to an entrée of grilled venison or pork chops (omit the confectioners' sugar in that case).

Serves 4

2 tablespoons melted butter

8 Buckwheat Crepes (recipe on page 00)

½ cup strawberry preserves

Confectioners' sugar for dusting

1. Coat a small sauté pan with ½ teaspoon of the butter over low heat. Place a cooked buckwheat crepe in the pan, browned side down, and heat through for 30 seconds.

2. Spread 1 tablespoon of the preserves onto the crepe. Fold the crepe in half twice to form a triangle. Remove from the pan, and keep warm.

3. Repeat with the remaining butter, crepes, and preserves.

4. To serve, place 2 crepes on each dessert plate, and dust with confectioners' sugar. ✱

Ricotta Crepe Soufflés with Fresh Raspberry Sauce

Michael Kalanty

✳

A very elegant way to end a meal—and, if the crepes have been made ahead and frozen, a very easy one at that! This recipe is intended as a dessert, but you could transform it into a stunning appetizer or luncheon entrée by omitting the sugar and orange zest from the filling and substituting some freshly cracked black pepper and 2 tablespoons of minced fresh herbs, such as basil, parsley, or cilantro; then serve the crepe soufflés with a little homemade tomato sauce instead of the raspberries.

Serves 4

Raspberry Sauce

1 pint fresh raspberries

½ teaspoon lime juice

2 tablespoon sugar

1 teaspoon red wine vinegar

Crepe Soufflés

1½ cups ricotta cheese (baking variety), at room temperature

⅔ cup plus 1 tablespoon sugar

⅛ teaspoon salt

1 teaspoon grated orange zest

3 large egg whites

⅛ teaspoon cream of tartar

8 Basic Crepes (recipe on page 143)

Raspberry Sauce

1. Place the raspberries in a small glass or ceramic bowl. Add the lime juice, sugar, and vinegar, and toss with a fork, bruising about a fourth of the berries to make a thick, chunky sauce. Cover, and set aside for 20 minutes.

Crepe Soufflés

2. Adjust the oven rack to the middle of the oven. Heat the oven to 375°F. Line a baking tray with parchment paper.

3. Place the cheese in a medium bowl. Stir in ⅓ cup of the sugar, the salt, and the orange zest.

4. In a medium stainless steel bowl, whisk the egg whites with the cream of tartar until soft peaks form. Add ⅓ cup of the sugar, and beat until firm peaks form.

5. Fold the egg whites into the cheese mixture by thirds.

6. Arrange the crepes on the baking tray. Spread the cheese filling over half of each crepe. Fold the other half of the crepe over to cover the filling. Sprinkle with the remaining tablespoon of sugar.

7. Bake 10 to 12 minutes, until the filling has risen and browned lightly and the edges of the crepes are crisp.

8. Immediately place 2 crepes on each dessert plate, and spoon the raspberry sauce over them. ✳

Individual Passion Fruit Soufflés

Greg Tompkins

✳

Keep a pot of ice water close at hand when cooking sugar. Burns from sugar are among the worst you can get in the kitchen. If you do get burned, plunge the affected area into the ice water for about a minute. This can save a world of hurt.

Serves 6

1¼ cups sugar

3 ounces water

1 cup pureed passion fruit

6 egg whites

1. Heat the oven to 375°F.

2. Combine the sugar and water in a small saucepan, and cook to the hard crack stage, 290°F on a candy thermometer.

3. While the sugar is cooking, heat the passion fruit in a small saucepan.

4. When the sugar reaches the hard crack stage, remove it from the heat, and, using hot mitts and a long-handled spoon, carefully stir in the fruit puree. The mixture will steam and sputter considerably.

5. Return the mixture to the heat, and cook it to the hard ball stage, 247°F, stirring frequently to prevent sticking and scorching.

6. When the fruit mixture reaches 220°F on the candy thermometer, start beating the egg whites in an electric mixer. They should form medium-stiff peaks exactly when the fruit mixture reaches the hard ball stage.

7. With the mixer running at high speed, very carefully pour the fruit mixture onto the egg whites, not onto the beaters (as it will splash and not be incorporated) or down the side of the bowl (as it will collect at the bottom and not be incorporated).

8. Let the mixture continue to whip at medium speed while you prepare 6 4-ounce soufflé dishes. Spread butter evenly over the interior of each dish; then fill the dish a third full of sugar. Turn the dish to coat the inside with sugar evenly all the way to the lip. Discard the excess sugar.

9. Spoon the soufflé mixture into the dishes, slightly overfilling each one. Level the mixture by scraping an icing spatula quickly across the rim of each dish.

10. Bake the soufflés for 15 to 20 minutes, until puffed and lightly browned. ✳

Frozen Chocolate Soufflé
(Soufflé Glacé)

Greg Tompkins

This soufflé is made from a Swiss meringue, the most dense and durable of meringues. It is simple to produce.
The only pitfall to avoid is cooking the egg whites while you dissolve the sugar. You stir the sugar and egg whites over
simmering water, and it is extremely important to keep the water bath below 180°F.

Raw eggs are an essential element in this recipe. If you wish to avoid them, you should probably stick with the hot soufflés.

Serves 8

9 ounces unsweetened chocolate, finely chopped

2 cups heavy cream

4 egg yolks

4 egg whites

1 cup sugar

3 tablespoons confectioners' sugar for decoration

1. Attach a wide strip of parchment or foil around the outside of a 1-quart soufflé dish, so that it forms a "collar" about 4 inches above the top of the dish. (If you prefer, make collars for 8 4-ounce soufflé cups, rising 2 inches above their rims.)

2. In the top of a medium double-boiler, melt the chocolate over simmering water. Add the cream, and combine.

3. Remove from the heat, and whip in the egg yolks, until the mixture is smooth and shiny. Set aside.

4. Combine the egg whites and sugar. Stir together over simmering water until the sugar has completely dissolved.

5. Place the egg white mixture in the bowl of a mixer, and whip until the meringue is thick and lukewarm.

6. Fold a third of the meringue into the chocolate mixture to loosen it. Then quickly fold in the remaining meringue.

7. When the mixture is homogeneous, pour it into the soufflé mold, filling the dish almost to the top of the collar.

8. Freeze the soufflé for at least 3 hours and up to 2 days.

9. To serve, remove the collar. Prepare a decorative stencil made from cardboard of cake-box or cereal-box thickness, and place it over the soufflé. Dust confectioners' sugar over the stencil, then lift the stencil carefully to leave a pattern on top of the soufflé. Serve. *

White Chocolate and Pistachio Bavarian with Chocolate Lace

Bo Friberg

✳

This elegant, towering dessert is actually much easier to assemble than it appears. However, you need to organize the components before you start, be gentle when applying the chocolate lace to the Bavarian, and get some experience in piping chocolate. An easier alternative is to spoon the Bavarian into individual serving dishes or glasses to set in the refrigerator, and then sprinkle the pistachios and fresh raspberries on top before serving.

Serves 16

Bavarian Filling

1/4 cup pistachio nuts

2 cups heavy cream

5 teaspoons unflavored gelatin powder

1/2 cup cold water

12 ounces white chocolate, cut into small pieces

2 tablespoons canning pectin powder (if unavailable, increase gelatin to 6 teaspoons instead)

1/2 cup sugar

4 egg whites

Lace and Garnishes

About 1/2 teaspoon light corn syrup

2 cups dark chocolate, tempered (recipe on page 151, or purchase coating chocolate, which does not require tempering) and melted

1 1/2 cups White Chocolate Sauce (recipe on page 151)

1/3 cup Bitter Chocolate Sauce (recipe on page 152)

4 cups small raspberries

1. Assemble 16 tubes 1¾ inches in diameter and 3 inches tall. (You can buy plastic tubing at a plastics or hobby supply store. Or you can make tubes by cutting 3-by-6¼-inch pieces of polyurethane or acetate, a heavy plastic, overlapping the short ends about ¼ inch, and taping them. This will give you a tube 1¾ inches in diameter.) Make sure the tubes stand up straight; if not, trim them as necessary.

2. Cut 16 rectangles of parchment paper 3 by 6 inches, and line the insides of the tubes with them. The paper will overlap inside about ½ inch. Stand the tubes on end on a sheet pan. Don't make the Bavarian filling until you have the tubes ready to fill, because it starts to set fairly quickly.

3. Blanch the pistachio nuts. Remove the skins, and chop the nuts coarsely. Reserve half of the nuts for decoration, choosing the better-looking pieces. Set the others aside for the filling.

4. Whip the cream until it forms soft peaks; do not overwhip. Cover, and set aside in the refrigerator.

5. Sprinkle the gelatin over the cold water, and set it aside to soften.

6. Melt the white chocolate in a medium bowl over simmering, not boiling, water, stirring constantly. Do not let the temperature go over 110°F, or the chocolate may become gritty and unusable. Set aside.

7. Combine the pectin powder and the sugar in a medium mixing bowl. Stir in the egg whites. Place the bowl over simmering water, and heat, stirring constantly with a whisk, until the mixture reaches 140°F. Remove from the heat, and immediately whip until the mixture has cooled completely and formed stiff peaks, making a meringue.

Continued on page 150

8. Place the gelatin mixture over simmering water, and heat to dissolve. Working quickly, first stir the gelatin mixture into the melted white chocolate. Then stir a third of the meringue into the chocolate mixture, to temper the meringue. Add this mixture to the remaining meringue. Stir in the chilled whipped cream and the nuts that were set aside for the filling.

9. Place the filling in a pastry bag with a number 6 plain tip. Pipe the filling into the 16 plastic tubes, filling them completely. Place the tubes (still on the sheet pan) in the refrigerator overnight, or in the freezer for at least 2 hours, to set.

10. While the Bavarians are chilling, cut 20 rectangles of parchment paper 4 by 5½ inches. You need only 16 but this gives you a few extra in case some lace pieces break. It is important that the width of the paper used to pipe the chocolate lace be the same size as the inside circumference of the tubes used for the Bavarians. The long edges of the lace can either miter together precisely or be slightly apart, but they must not overlap even slightly or the lace will break when the paper is removed.

11. To make piping chocolate, add the corn syrup, one drop at a time, to the melted chocolate, until the chocolate thickens slightly and will hold its shape when piped.

12. Remove the chilled Bavarians from their tubes. Peel off the papers, and set the Bavarians aside in the refrigerator.

13. Place 2 of the parchment paper rectangles slightly apart on a full sheet of parchment paper. Place roughly ¼ cup of the piping chocolate in a piping bag. (Use a large enough bag and enough chocolate to complete 2 papers of lace without refilling.) Cut a small opening in the bag. Pipe a straight line along 1 long edge of 1 rectangle. Then pipe a zigzag pattern diagonally over the rectangle, first in one diagonal direction and then in the opposite diagonal direction, spacing the lines about ¼ inch apart and extending the lines out onto the larger sheet of paper on all sides. Repeat on the second rectangle of paper.

14. As soon as you finish piping on the second rectangle of paper, lift up the first one, without disturbing the chocolate except that the edges of the chocolate will break cleanly at the edges of the paper rectangle. Remove 1 Bavarian from the refrigerator. With the paper rectangle of chocolate lace lying before you with the straight line at the top, place the Bavarian on top of the lace at the left edge of the rectangle of paper, even with the bottom of the lace, so that 1 inch of lace (including the straight line) extends above the Bavarian. Roll the chocolate lace paper snugly around the Bavarian, so that the chocolate lace and the

rectangle of paper stick to the Bavarian, and line up the left and right edges of the lace (but do not overlap them). Stand the Bavarian on end. Repeat with the second rectangle of paper and another chilled Bavarian.

15. Repeat steps 13–14 for all the servings of Bavarian. Set aside in the refrigerator with the papers attached, until ready to serve.

16. To serve, carefully peel the paper away from a serving of Bavarian. Stand the Bavarian on end, off-center, on a dessert plate. Use a plastic squeeze bottle to pipe dots of White Chocolate Sauce the size of a quarter, very slightly apart, in a half-circle in front of the Bavarian at the edge of the base of the plate. Pipe a much smaller dot of Bitter Chocolate Sauce in the center of each white dot. Drag a wooden skewer through the chocolate dots in a wavy pattern to create a series of hearts. Place about 12 small raspberries on top of the dessert inside the chocolate lace "basket." Sprinkle 3 to 4 raspberries between the dessert and the sauce. Sprinkle some of the reserved pistachio nuts around the raspberries. *

Tempered Chocolate

Heat chocolate to 120°F. Pour it onto a marble surface, and cool it to between 75°F and 80°F. Scrape it into the top of a double boiler, and heat over simmering water until it is just under 90°F, or the temperature specified by the manufacturer for its particular chocolate. *

White Chocolate Sauce

1 cup water

1¹/4 cups sugar

¹/2 cup light corn syrup

1 pound, 4 ounces white chocolate, melted (see step 6 on page 148)

1. Combine the water, sugar, and corn syrup in a saucepan, and bring the syrup to a boil.

2. Remove from the heat, add the melted chocolate, and stir until combined. If the sauce is not completely smooth, strain it before serving. (Yield: 4 cups.) *

Continued on page 152

Bitter Chocolate Sauce

2 cups water

1/4 cup sugar

1/2 cup light corn syrup

1 cup unsweetened cocoa powder

14 ounces dark sweet chocolate, melted

2 ounces unsweetened chocolate, melted

1. Combine the water, sugar, and corn syrup in a saucepan. Bring to a boil, then remove from the heat.

2. In a medium saucepan add enough of the sugar mixture to the cocoa powder to make a soft paste, stirring until the mixture is completely smooth. Gradually add the remaining sugar mixture.

3. Add both of the melted chocolates, and stir until combined. If the sauce is not completely smooth, strain it before serving. (Yield: 4 cups.) ∗

Orange Soufflés with Grand Marnier

Tamara Frey

٭

Here is a bright dessert presentation, light, yet intensely flavored.
Lemon (or Cardamom or Almond) Wafers (recipe on page 172) make a nice accompaniment.

Serves 6

6 large oranges

½ cup concentrated orange juice

2 tablespoons Grand Marnier
(orange liqueur)

5 egg whites

1½ tablespoons sugar

1. Heat the oven to 350°F.

2. Cut the tops off the oranges. Cut just enough off the bottoms so that the oranges can stand. With a paring knife and a sharp teaspoon, scoop out enough orange pulp to create a bowl in the shell. Be careful not to pierce the bottoms or sides of the shells. Some orange pulp may remain.

3. Squeeze and strain the scooped out pulp. Combine 1 cup of the strained fresh juice with the concentrated juice, and bring to a boil in a small saucepan. Boil until the liquid is reduced to half, and a very thick syrup is formed.

4. Add 1 tablespoon of the Grand Marnier. Remove from the heat, and cool slightly.

5. Whip the egg whites until soft peaks form. Add the sugar, and whip until stiff peaks form. Fold a little of the egg whites into the orange syrup. Then fold the syrup into the rest of the egg whites.

6. Into each empty orange shell, put ½ teaspoon of the remaining Grand Marnier. Fill the shells with the soufflé mixture. (The filling can go above the rim.)

7. Bake for 8 to 10 minutes, until golden.

8. Serve 1 shell per person. ٭

Cappuccino Mousse with Sambuca Cream in a Chocolate Cup

Bo Friberg

✳

Of the many ways to present a mousse, this is about as fancy as it gets! There is, of course, a price to pay in the many steps required to complete this dessert, but modifications are possible without sacrificing all of the aesthetics or any of the flavor. The easiest variation is to leave out the chocolate coffee cups altogether, and serve the mousse in pretty stemmed glasses. But if you want to give the chocolate cups a try (they are really fairly easy) you can still omit the handles, which take more experience than the cups, and make chocolate "bowls" instead.

Serves 16

Cappuccino Mousse

3 cups heavy cream

6 egg yolks

1/3 cup honey

1/4 cup coffee liqueur

10 ounces dark sweet chocolate

4 ounces unsweetened chocolate

Cups

16 Chocolate Coffee Cups
(recipe on page 156)

1/4 cup Sambuca liqueur
(anise-flavored liqueur)

1 cup heavy cream

4 cups Pastry Cream Mousseline Sauce
(recipe on page 196)

3 teaspoons finely ground coffee

16 Cookie Spoons
(recipe on page 157)

16 edible flowers

Cappuccino Mousse

1. In a medium bowl, whip the cream until it forms soft peaks. Set aside.

2. In a large bowl, whip the egg yolks until they form a smooth ribbon when dropped from a spoon.

3. In a small saucepan, heat the honey until it just starts to boil, then immediately whip the honey into the egg yolks, thoroughly scraping all of the honey out of the pan. Continue whipping until the mixture is cold.

4. Stir in the liqueur.

5. In a medium double boiler melt the 2 chocolates together.

6. Rapidly incorporate the melted chocolates into the egg mixture.

7. Fold in the whipped cream. Set aside in the refrigerator until you are ready to start serving preparations.

8. Just before serving time, soften the mousse to a pipable consistency, if necessary, by stirring it briefly in a double boiler over hot water. Place the mousse in a pastry bag with a number 7 plain tip.

Cups

9. Pipe the mousse into the chocolate cups, and form smooth mounds on the tops. Set aside in the refrigerator for up to 1 hour, while you finish preparing to serve.

Continued on page 156

10. Add the liqueur to the cream, and whip until it forms soft peaks. Set aside in the refrigerator.

11. Pour in ¼ cup of the mousseline sauce in the center of each dessert plate. Use the back of a spoon to shape the sauce into a 5-inch circle resembling a saucer. Sift the coffee lightly over the sauce.

12. Spoon a large dollop of whipped Sambuca cream on top of the mousse in each chocolate cup.

13. Hold a Cookie Spoon by the handle, and gently push the bowl of the spoon partway into the cream. Leave some of the bowl showing. Place an edible flower next to the spoon.

14. Wearing latex gloves, to avoid leaving fingerprints, place a chocolate cup in the center of each plate, giving it a careful twist to ensure it will not slide in the sauce. *

Chocolate Coffee Cups

About 16 ounces tempered dark sweet chocolate (recipe on page 151) (or dark coating chocolate, which does not need to be tempered)

1 tablespoon vegetable oil

About 3 drops corn syrup

1. In a medium double boiler, melt the chocolate over simmering water until it is just above body temperature (about 100°F), no hotter.

2. Blow up 16 small balloons until they measure 3½ inches in diameter at a point 2 inches from the round end of the balloon (about the size of a large orange).

3. After tying the balloons, use your hand to squeeze the top of the balloon toward the bottom to stretch the rubber evenly. (If there is a small area of thicker rubber at the bottom, it will absorb more oil and stick to the chocolate.)

4. Lightly coat the bottom 2½ inches of the balloons with the vegetable oil by rubbing it on with your hand. Do not use too much oil or the chocolate won't adhere; excess oil can also run back into the remaining chocolate supply and ruin it.

5. Line 2 sheet pans with parchment paper, and set extra sheets of parchment on a work surface.

6. Push the round end of 1 balloon 2 inches deep into the chocolate, holding the balloon straight, and cover the bottom with chocolate. Lift the balloon, and let the excess chocolate drip back into the pot. Scrape the bottom of the balloon against the edge of the pot to remove more excess chocolate. Blot the bottom on a sheet of parchment paper, and then carefully set the dipped balloon on the lined sheet pan.

7. Repeat step 6 with the rest of the balloons.

8. Place the sheet pan holding the cups in the refrigerator for 2 minutes, to set the chocolate.

9. Puncture the balloons with a toothpick at the top, next to where they are tied, and set them aside to release the air slowly. Once the balloons have deflated, remove and discard them.

10. If necessary, warm a metal spatula, and smooth the top edges of the cups by pressing the flat side of the spatula gently against them.

11. Add the corn syrup, 1 drop at a time, to about $1/3$ cup of the remaining melted chocolate, to thicken it just enough so it will hold its shape when piped. Place a portion of the mixture in a piping bag, cut a small opening, and pipe out 16 handle shapes on the second lined sheet pan, refilling the bag as needed. Place the pan in the refrigerator for 1 minute to harden the handles.

12. Wearing latex gloves, to prevent fingerprints on the chocolate, remove the handles from the paper, quickly dip the ends in the melted chocolate mixture, and attach the handles to the sides of the cups.

13. Store the cups at room temperature (close to 60°F) until ready to use. They will keep for up to 5 days. (Yield: 16 chocolate cups.) ✳

Cookie Spoons

About $1/2$ cup Vanilla Tulip Paste
(recipe on page 197)

$1/2$ teaspoon unsweetened cocoa powder

1. Make a spoon-shaped stencil using $1/16$-inch-thick cardboard.

2. Heat the oven to 425°F. Grease and flour the backs of 4 clean, even sheet pans (or use silicon mats, which do not need to be greased and floured). Tap the pans to remove excess flour.

3. In a small dish, color 1 tablespoon of the tulip paste with the cocoa powder. Place the cocoa-colored paste in a piping bag, and cut a small opening.

4. Place the spoon stencil on 1 of the prepared sheet pans (or silicon mats). Place some of the plain tulip paste inside the stencil, and spread it evenly to fill the shape. Lift the stencil, and place it on another area of the pan. Repeat to make 16 spoons, placing no more than 4 per pan.

5. Pipe small decorative dots of the cocoa-colored paste in the handle of each spoon.

Continued on page 158

6. Bake one pan at a time for about 4 minutes, until a few light brown spots appear on the cookies.

7. Leave the pan in the oven, and remove the cookie spoons one at a time, choosing the spoon that looks most done each time. Leave the oven on. Working quickly, center each cookie over 1 metal spoon of about the same size, place a second metal spoon on top, and press the metal spoons gently to shape the bowl of the cookie spoon.

8. Repeat steps 6–7 to bake and form the remaining spoons.

9. Store the cookie spoons in an airtight container at room temperature, until ready to use. They will keep for several days. ✳

Flaming Rum Bananas with Meringue

Tamara Frey

✶

This dessert was created in Maui, where the trees are laden with "hands" of bananas.
Many varieties of bananas exist. Experiment with different kinds in this dish.
Serve the dessert with Lemon Wafers (recipe on page 172), if you wish.

Serves 6

Banana Filling

2 teaspoons unsalted butter

8 firm, ripe, medium bananas,
coarsely chopped

2 tablespoons sweetener
(white or brown sugar, maple syrup,
honey, or sucanat—an organic cane sugar)

5 tablespoons rum

1 tablespoon fresh lime juice

Meringue

5 egg whites

2 tablespoons sugar

1 teaspoon rum

1/2 teaspoon vanilla extract

Banana Filling

1. Heat the oven to 300°F. Butter 6 1-cup ramekins with unsalted butter.

2. In a large sauté pan, heat the butter, and sauté the bananas for 1 minute.

3. Stir in the sweetener, and sauté 3 to 5 minutes more, depending on the variety of banana, until the bananas are soft.

4. Pour in the rum. Remove the pan from the heat, tilt it to catch the flame (if you don't have a gas stove, light a match to the rum), and flambé the bananas. Simmer a few seconds, until the alcohol burns off.

5. Add the lime juice. Adjust the seasonings, if necessary, with more sweetener or lime juice.

6. Distribute the banana mixture evenly among the ramekins.

Meringue

7. Whip the egg whites until they form soft peaks. Slowly add the sugar, rum, and vanilla. Whip until stiff peaks form.

8. Spoon the meringue on top of the banana mixture. Bake for 15 minutes, until the meringue is golden and cooked through. ✶

Fruit Baskets

Bo Friberg

This is a less-caloric version of a dessert made in Sweden years ago for Easter, in which the baskets were filled with small, handmade marzipan Easter eggs rather than raspberries. In those days there certainly were no fresh raspberries to be had at that time of year, as importing fresh out-of-season produce from all over the globe was not commonplace the way it is today.

Serves 16

4 cups Vanilla Tulip Paste
(recipe on page 197)

2 teaspoons unsweetened cocoa powder

About 1 tablespoon heavy cream

1/4 cup sour cream

1 white sponge cake (or angel food cake)
(your favorite recipe, or purchased)

3/4 cup whipped cream

4 cups Raspberry Sauce
(recipe on page 163)

4 cups fresh raspberries

16 mint sprigs

1. Make a 1¾-by-9-inch rectangular stencil from 1/16-inch-thick cardboard, to use in making the basket sides. Save the cardboard rectangle you cut out of the middle of the stencil, and overlap the short edges ¼ inch to make a tube. Tape together. Bend the round tube to make an oval.

2. Make a ½-by-10-inch stencil from 1/16-inch-thick cardboard, to use in making the basket handles.

3. Heat the oven to 425°F. Lightly grease and flour the backs of 8 even sheet pans (or use silicon mats, which do not need to be greased and floured). Shake off the excess flour. If you do not have 8 pans, clean the pans between batches, and grease and flour them again.

4. In a small bowl, mix 3 tablespoons of the tulip paste with the cocoa powder. Put a portion of it into a piping bag, cut a small opening, and set aside. (Refill the bag as needed.)

5. Place the basket stencil on one of the prepared sheet pans. Spread some of the plain tulip paste smoothly and evenly inside the stencil. Lift the stencil, and place it on another area of the pan. Make 4 rectangles on each of 4 pans.

6. Pipe 2 lines of cocoa-colored tulip paste the length of the basket rectangle and evenly spaced across the width.

7. Bake one pan at a time for about 6 minutes, until the first rectangle begins to show light brown spots. Leave the pan in the oven with the door open and the oven on.

8. Working quickly, remove the rectangle with the most brown color, and wrap it around the cardboard oval. Overlap the ends, and press them down hard against the work surface to weld them together. Slide the cookie basket off the cardboard, and set it aside, standing up.

Continued on page 162

9. Repeat steps 7–8, until you have made 16 baskets. Set them aside.

10. Place the handle stencil on a prepared sheet pan, and spread plain tulip paste smoothly and evenly inside it. Make 5 on each of 4 pans. (It's a good idea to make a few extra handles, since they break easily.) Pipe a line of cocoa-colored tulip paste the length of the strip in the center of each handle.

11. Place a rolling pin with a 4-inch diameter on a sheet pan or on your work surface. Raise both ends of the rolling pin a few inches, and anchor the pin so that it will not roll, using a handful of dough (or similar material) to do both.

12. Bake the tulip paste handle strips one pan at a time, for about 4 minutes, until they begin to color.

13. Remove them, and drape them over the rolling pin. Hold the ends against the pin for a few seconds until firm. Then lift up the rolling pin, and carefully pull the handles off. Set them aside. Bake and form the remaining handles the same way.

14. Gradually mix enough heavy cream into the sour cream to make it the same consistency as the raspberry sauce. Refrigerate, covered, until ready to use.

15. Cut out 16 oval pieces of the sponge cake that will fit snugly inside the oval baskets. Cover and set aside.

16. Place the whipped cream in a pastry bag with a medium plain tip. Set aside in the refrigerator.

17. When you are ready to serve, place a cake oval in the bottom of each cookie basket. Pipe whipped cream on top, filling to just below the rim. Place a handle on the basket, carefully pushing the ends into the cream to secure them. Top the cream with the raspberries.

18. Place each basket off-center on a dessert plate. Pour a small pool of raspberry sauce in front of the basket, and shape the pool to curve toward the sides of the basket, using the back of a spoon.

19. Place some of the sour cream mixture in a piping bag (or plastic squeeze bottle). Cut a small opening in the bag. Pipe large dots of the mixture (about the size of a nickel) in a curved line in the center of the raspberry sauce. Drag a small wooden skewer through the dots to make curved hearts. Decorate each basket with a mint sprig. Serve immediately *

Raspberry Sauce

About 2½ cups fresh (or thawed frozen) raspberries

About 1½ tablespoons cornstarch

Sugar to taste

1. Puree the raspberries in a food processor until smooth. Strain the puree to remove the seeds. Measure the puree.

2. Measure 1½ tablespoons of the cornstarch for each 2 cups of puree into a medium saucepan. Mix in enough puree to liquefy the cornstarch. Then stir in the remaining puree.

3. Heat the sauce to a simmer. Taste, and add sugar if needed. Simmer the sauce for about 3 minutes, then let it cool. Thin the sauce with water if necessary.

4. Store the sauce, covered, in the refrigerator, until needed. It will keep for up to 4 days. (Yield: 2 cups.) *

Spiced Pear Cobbler

Michael Kalanty

The unusual, spicy combination of ginger and vinegar gives an updated taste to this classic American comfort dessert of baked pears topped with a tender biscuit dough. Try this garnished with ice cream. It makes a perfect fall finale to a dinner spotlighting regional American specialties.

Serves 4

Pears

2 teaspoons unsalted butter

3 pounds pears (Bartlett or Bosc), peeled, halved, and cored

2 tablespoons rice wine vinegar (or sherry vinegar)

Grated zest of 1 orange

1/8 teaspoon salt

1 teaspoon grated fresh ginger

1/2 teaspoon ground cardamom

1 teaspoon ground cinnamon

1/2 teaspoon ground cloves

2 tablespoons cornstarch

1/3 cup loosely packed light brown sugar

1/3 cup granulated sugar (or more to taste)

Topping

1 1/2 cups all-purpose flour

4 tablespoons granulated sugar

2 teaspoons baking powder

1/2 teaspoon baking soda

Pears

1. Adjust the oven rack to the middle of the oven. Heat the oven to 375°F. Butter a 9-inch square baking dish with the unsalted butter, and set aside.

2. Slice the pears lengthwise 1/4 inch thick. Place the slices in a large stainless steel bowl, and toss immediately with the vinegar, to prevent browning.

3. Add the remaining ingredients for the pears, and toss well. Allow the mixture to sit at room temperature, covered, for 20 minutes.

4. Taste the pears and add granulated sugar if necessary. Transfer the mixture to the buttered baking dish. Bake it for 20 minutes.

Topping

5. While the pear mixture is baking, sift the flour, 3 tablespoons of the sugar, the baking powder, baking soda, and salt into a medium bowl. Add the butter, and cut it in with a fork or pastry cutter, until the mixture is crumbly and resembles coarse meal.

6. Add the buttermilk, and mix with a wooden spoon just until the dry ingredients are moistened.

7. Stir the mixture lightly for 1 minute more, adding a little more flour if the dough sticks to the spoon.

8. Remove the pear mixture from the oven. Pinch off pieces of the topping dough about 1 tablespoon in size, and place them on top of the fruit. Lightly press the dough down with the back of a large spoon to level the top. Sprinkle with the remaining tablespoon of sugar. Immediately return the cobbler to the oven.

1 teaspoon salt

6 tablespoons unsalted butter, chilled

¾ cup buttermilk (or plain yogurt)

9. Bake for another 20 to 25 minutes, until the topping is browned and cooked through, and the pears are tender when pierced with a knife.

10. Remove from the oven, and cool on a rack. Serve warm or completely cooled. ✳

Peaches Poached in Sauternes with Mascarpone

Michael Kalanty

Here's an elegant pairing of luscious wine-imbued fruit with creamy, sweetened cheese.
Crisp cookies accompany this dessert for the ultimate complement in texture.

Serves 8

2 cups Sauternes

2 quarts plus 2 cups water

1 lemon, sliced with skin on

1/2 cup plus 2 1/2 tablespoons sugar

8 black peppercorns

4 firm, underripe peaches (preferably white)

6 ounces mascarpone

1/4 cup heavy cream

1/2 pint fresh raspberries

2 teaspoons fresh lemon juice

8 Palmiers (recipe on page 174)
or Browned Butter Cigarette Cookies
(recipe on page 177) (optional)

1. In a medium saucepan, combine the Sauternes, 2 cups of water, lemon, 1/2 cup of sugar, and peppercorns. Simmer for 10 minutes.

2. Meanwhile, bring the remaining 2 quarts of water to a boil in a medium saucepan. Add the peaches, and boil for 1 minute. Remove with a slotted spoon, and hold under cold water for 2 minutes.

3. Carefully peel off the peach skins, using your fingers or the back of a paring knife. Cut the peaches in half, and remove the pits.

4. Place the peaches in the simmering Sauternes mixture. Cut a circle of parchment paper to fit inside the pot and place the parchment over the peaches, so that they baste as they poach.

5. Poach at a bare simmer, turning occasionally, for 7 to 10 minutes, until the peaches are just tender when pierced with a knife.

6. Carefully lift the peaches from the liquid with a slotted spoon. Set them on a plate, cover them with the parchment circle, and allow them to cool.

7. Bring the poaching liquid to a boil. Cook until it is reduced by half and just slightly syrupy. Remove from the stove, and cool to room temperature. Strain the liquid, and discard the lemon and pepper.

8. Transfer the peaches to a glass or ceramic bowl just large enough to hold them. Pour the cooled poaching liquid over them. Cover, and refrigerate for 4 hours.

9. While the peaches chill, combine the mascarpone and cream in a medium stainless steel bowl. Stir gently for about 30 seconds, until the mixture is homogeneous. Sprinkle in 1 1/2 tablespoons of the remaining sugar, and stir for 30 seconds more. Cover, and refrigerate until ready to serve.

10. In a small bowl, combine the raspberries with the remaining tablespoon of sugar and the lemon juice. Toss to mix well. Cover, and refrigerate until ready to serve.

11. To serve, spoon the poaching liquid onto 8 dessert plates. Place a peach half on each plate. Pipe or spoon a dollop of mascarpone next to the peach. Garnish with the raspberries. If desired, add a Palmier or Browned Butter Cigarette Cookie. *

Raspberry-Cassis Sorbet

Michael Kalanty

✳

Sorbet is an ingenious way to transform slightly overripe fruit into a light and refreshing finale to an elegant meal.
This method eliminates the need for an ice-cream churn. Present sorbet in wine or champagne glasses with
crisp accompaniments such as Browned Butter Cigarette Cookies (recipe on page 177) or Palmiers (recipe on page 174).

Serves 6

1 cup water

½ cup sugar

2 cups fresh raspberries

⅓ cup crème de cassis
(black currant liqueur)

2 tablespoons fresh lemon juice

1 egg white

Fresh mint leaves

1. Combine the water and sugar in a small saucepan, and boil for 1 minute. Cool to room temperature.

2. Add the raspberries, crème de cassis, and lemon juice to the sugar syrup, and let stand for 1 hour.

3. Strain the syrup, and press the raspberries against the strainer to puree them and remove the seeds. Allow the puree to strain into the sugar syrup. Taste the mixture, and add a little more sugar or lemon if it is too tart or too sweet.

4. Pour the mixture into ice cube trays or a nonreactive pan, and freeze it overnight. (It will not freeze completely.)

5. Place half of the frozen mixture in a food processor, and pulse for 10 seconds. Lightly beat the egg white, and add half to the mixture. Process for about 15 seconds; remove. Repeat with the remaining half of the raspberry mixture and egg white.

6. Pack the sorbet into a small metal or plastic container. Place a layer of plastic wrap directly on the surface of the sorbet, and another layer over the top of the container. Refreeze for up to 30 minutes before serving.

7. Scoop into glasses, garnish with mint leaves, and serve. ✳

Mille-Feuilles with Seasonal Fruit

Michael Kalanty

⁎

A classic of the French pastry repertoire, mille-feuilles means "a thousand leaves," referring to the flaky layers of baked puff pastry that encase a luscious filling. This rendition features fresh fruits accented with a mousseline sauce—a pastry cream lightened with whipped cream. Mille-feuilles make a truly dramatic and impressive dessert, belying the ease with which they are assembled.

Serves 9

16 ounces frozen puff pastry dough, defrosted in refrigerator

⅓ cup sugar

1 egg white, lightly beaten

4 cups assorted seasonal fruit (such as mango, pineapple, and kiwi), cut crosswise into ⅛-inch to ¼-inch slices

3 cups Pastry Cream Mousseline Sauce (recipe on page 196)

1. Heat the oven to 400°F. Line a baking sheet with parchment paper.

2. Roll the pastry into 2 squares, each slightly larger than 12 by 12 inches and ⅛ inch thick. Refrigerate for 20 minutes; then cut each square into 4-inch squares. (Yield: 18.)

3. Using a spatula, so as not to stretch the squares, transfer half of them to the lined baking sheet.

4. Invert a lightweight cooling rack on top of the squares so the dough will rise evenly during baking.

5. Bake for 12 minutes, until the dough is puffed and lightly browned. Reduce the heat to 375°F. Remove the rack, sprinkle the tops of the squares with one-fourth of the sugar, and bake for 15 minutes more.

6. Remove the baking sheet from the oven. Invert the squares, brush the new tops with half of the egg white, and sprinkle one-fourth of the sugar over them. Bake for 5 to 7 minutes more, until the dough is firm and cooked through. Remove the squares from the sheet, and cool them on a rack.

7. Increase the oven temperature to 400°F again, and repeat steps 3–6 with the remaining dough, sugar, and egg white. (You may wrap the cooled mille-feuilles in plastic and store them at room temperature for up to 2 days. Crisp them in a 350°F oven for 3 to 4 minutes, and cool them before using.)

8. To assemble the mille-feuilles, place 1 pastry square in the center of a plate. Arrange the slices of fruit decoratively over the square. Spoon about 3 tablespoons of the mousseline sauce over the rear third of the square, spilling onto the plate. Offset another pastry square, at an angle from the bottom square and tilting up toward the front, on top of the sauce. ⁎

Crystallized Ginger Biscotti

Johnathan Robinette

The classic dipping cookie is given a new twist with fresh lime juice and a mysterious note from crystallized ginger.

Serves 36

½ pound (2 sticks) butter, softened

2 cups sugar

Grated zest of 4 limes

¾ teaspoon salt

2 tablespoons vanilla extract

4 eggs

4 cups flour

1 teaspoon baking powder

¼ teaspoon baking soda

4 tablespoons lime juice

2 tablespoons crystallized ginger, crushed

½ cup heavy cream

1. Place the butter in a large mixer bowl, and beat at low speed for 1 minute, until light and fluffy.

2. With the mixer running, slowly add the sugar and lime zest, and beat until well incorporated. Add the salt and vanilla, and beat to incorporate. Add the eggs, one at a time, and continue to beat. Scrape down the sides as needed. Set aside.

3. In a medium bowl, sift together the flour, baking powder, and baking soda.

4. Using the paddle attachment, slowly stir the flour mixture into the butter mixture. Add the lime juice and ginger, and mix. While mixing, slowly add the cream until the mixture forms a soft dough. Transfer the dough to a pastry bag with a medium plain tip.

5. Line a sheet pan with aluminum foil. Form the dough into 2 loaves by piping 4 even lines of dough side by side, crosswise on the pan, for each loaf. Cover with plastic wrap, and refrigerate for 12 hours (or overnight).

6. Heat the oven to 350°F.

7. Remove the sheet pan from the refrigerator, and bake for 10 to 12 minutes, until the loaves are brown and a toothpick inserted in the center comes out clean. Reduce the oven temperature to 300°F.

8. Cool the loaves on a rack until they are cool to the touch. Slice them crosswise into ½-inch-thick slices. Place the slices, upright and slightly apart, back on the baking sheet.

9. Bake the biscotti at 300°F for 12 to 15 minutes more, until they are lightly browned and crisp. Remove the biscotti from the pan, and cool them on a rack. Store them in an airtight container at room temperature until needed. (Yield: about 6 dozen.) ✳

Lemon Wafers

Tamara Frey

✳

These wafers are high in flavor and low in fat. Enjoy!

Serves 6

1 cup pastry flour
(white or whole wheat)

¼ teaspoon baking powder

¼ teaspoon baking soda

2 tablespoons sweetener (sugar, maple
syrup, or sucanat—an organic cane sugar)

1 tablespoon grated lemon zest

1½ tablespoons unsalted butter

1 tablespoon lemon juice

4 tablespoons fruit juice
(apple, grape, or orange)

1. Heat the oven to 350°F. Butter a baking sheet.

2. Mix together the flour, baking powder, baking soda, and sweet-
    ener. Add the lemon zest.

3. Cut the butter into pea-size pieces, and add it to the mixture,
    rubbing the butter between your hands to blend.

4. Add the lemon juice and fruit juice a little at a time until the
    dough is the right consistency to roll out. Be careful not to
    handle the dough too much.

5. Roll the dough out to ¼ inch thick between 2 pieces of plastic
    wrap, flouring the sides of the dough and turning as you go.

6. With a biscuit cutter (or a diamond- or star-shaped cookie
    cutter), cut out the cookies and arrange them on the baking
    sheet.

7. Bake for 6 to 8 minutes, until golden. ✳

Variation: Cardamom Wafers

Omit the lemon zest and lemon juice. Increase the fruit juice
to 5 tablespoons. Add ½ teaspoon ground cardamom in step 2.

Variation: Almond Wafers

Omit the lemon zest and lemon juice. Increase the fruit juice
to 5 tablespoons. Add ⅛ teaspoon almond extract in step 4.

Vanilla Shortbread

Teresa Douglas / Mitchell

✻

Shortbread is one of the simplest cookies to make, and it freezes beautifully. It can look quite sophisticated when cut into pretty shapes and dusted with sugar. You can combine vanilla and chocolate shortbread to create an impressive marbled effect or to make pinwheel cookies.

Serves 12

16 tablespoons (2 sticks) butter

2/3 cup confectioners' sugar

1 teaspoon vanilla extract

2 cups flour

1/4 teaspoon salt

Granulated or confectioners' sugar for garnish

1. Heat the oven to 350°F.

2. Chop the butter into small pieces, and place it in a food processor. Add the confectioners' sugar and vanilla.

3. Sift the flour and salt over the butter mixture. Process until a soft round ball of dough is formed.

4. Chill the dough for 45 minutes, until it is firm but workable. Roll it out between 2 sheets of plastic wrap (or on a floured work surface) until it is 1/4 to 3/8 inch thick. Cut it into shapes or press it into a shortbread mold. Place the shortbread on an ungreased cookie sheet.

5. Bake for about 20 minutes, until cooked but not brown.

6. Cool on a rack. When the cookies are cool, dust them with the granulated or confectioners' sugar. (Yield: 24 1 1/2-ounce cookies.) ✻

Variation: Chocolate Shortbread

Reduce the flour to 1 3/4 cups. Add 1/2 cup unsweetened cocoa powder in step 3.

Palmiers

Michael Kalanty

✳

Sweet, buttery, and crisp! These cookies are great on their own and can transform a simple scoop of ice cream into a textural pleasure. Named for their resemblance to the furling leaves of the palm tree, these classics of the French pâtisserie are easily prepared and can be stored for several days. Commercially prepared puff pastry dough makes your work even simpler.

Serves 18

12 ounces frozen puff pastry dough, defrosted in refrigerator

About 1 cup sugar

1 large egg, lightly beaten

1. Heat the oven to 400°F. Line a baking tray with parchment paper.

2. Dust the puff pastry lightly with flour and roll it into a 12-by-18-inch rectangle, ⅛ inch thick. Brush the excess flour from the dough and the work surface.

3. Sprinkle ⅓ cup of the sugar on the work table. Place the puff pastry on top. Sprinkle another ⅓ cup of the sugar over the dough. Press the sugar into the pastry by rolling lightly with a rolling pin.

4. Fold both long edges of the dough in to the center. Sprinkle with a little more sugar, and press lightly with the rolling pin to seal the dough.

5. Repeat step 4.

6. Brush half of the dough lengthwise with the egg. Fold the dough in half and press tightly to secure the seam.

7. Cut the dough crosswise into ½-inch slices. Place the slices, cut side up, on the baking tray, spaced about 2 inches apart.

8. Place the tray in the oven, and reduce the temperature to 375°F. Bake 8 to 10 minutes, until the bottoms of the cookies are caramelized. Flip the cookies over, and bake until the new bottoms are caramelized and the dough is cooked throughout.

9. Remove from the oven, and cool on a rack. Loosen the cookies from the tray while they are slightly warm. Allow them to cool completely before storing. They will keep in an airtight container for up to 4 days. (Yield: about 3 dozen cookies.) ✳

Sacristains

Michael Kalanty

✳

These crisp cookies are coated in almond-sugar and twisted into a spiral shape.
Their resemblance to the liturgical corkscrew of ecclesiastical service lent them their name.

Serves 8

13 ounces frozen puff pastry dough, defrosted in refrigerator

½ cup sliced, blanched almonds

½ cup sugar

1 large egg, lightly beaten

1. Heat the oven to 400°F.

2. Dust the puff pastry lightly with flour, and roll it out into a 12-inch square. Cut the square in half. Cover with plastic wrap, and refrigerate for 20 minutes on a baking tray.

3. While the pastry chills, process the almonds and sugar together in a food processor until finely ground. (Do not overprocess the mixture or it will become gummy.)

4. Working with one piece of the pastry, brush the top with some of the egg. Sprinkle ¼ of the almond mixture over the dough, and press it into the pastry by rolling lightly with a rolling pin. Turn the pastry over and repeat the procedure on the other side.

5. Cut the pastry crosswise into ¾-inch strips.

6. Line a baking tray with parchment paper. Brush 2 strips of egg wash lengthwise on the parchment paper, 6 inches apart. Twist a strip of pastry into a corkscrew, and secure the ends to the parchment paper by pressing them into the strips of egg wash at the top and bottom. Repeat with the remaining strips of pastry. Refrigerate the formed strips for 20 minutes before baking.

7. Repeat steps 4–6 with the other half of the pastry and the almond mixture.

8. Place both trays in the oven, and reduce the temperature to 375°F. Bake for about 10 minutes, until lightly browned. Loosen the cookies, and flip them. Continue baking for 10 to 12 minutes more, until the cookies are golden brown and the dough is cooked throughout.

9. Cool the cookies on a rack. They will keep in an airtight container for up to 4 days. (Yield: 16 cookies.) ✳

Browned Butter Cigarette Cookies

Michael Kalanty

Browning the butter gives these crisp, fragile, rolled cookies even more elegance.
They make a great addition to a tea selection and a wonderful accompaniment to ice creams and sorbets.

Serves 8

4 ounces unsalted butter

½ teaspoon fresh lemon juice

4 large egg whites

⅞ cup sugar

1 cup all-purpose flour

2 teaspoons water

1. Heat the oven to 375°F.

2. Melt the butter in a small sauté pan over low heat, stirring with a wooden spoon. Allow the butter to bubble and start to darken, stirring continuously. When it turns medium brown and begins to smell nutlike, remove the pan from the heat.

3. Stir the lemon juice into the butter carefully. (It will spatter.) Set aside, and cool to room temperature.

4. Beat the egg whites until soft peaks form. Gradually add the sugar, and beat until stiff peaks form.

5. Beat the flour gradually into the egg white mixture. Stir in the cooled browned butter and the water.

6. Draw 6 3½-by-2½-inch ovals on a piece of parchment paper. Invert a baking tray, and place the paper, ink side down, on the back.

7. Place 2 teaspoons of batter in each oval. Spread the batter evenly to fill the oval shapes, using a small spatula or spoon dipped in cold water.

8. Bake the cookies for 7 to 8 minutes, until the ovals are evenly golden with browned edges.

9. Remove the tray from the oven, and immediately peel the cookies from the parchment. Roll them around a small dowel or pencil. Slide them off, and set them aside to cool completely.

10. Repeat steps 7–9 with the remaining batter. Add more water, a teaspoon at a time, if the batter stiffens.

11. When they are cool, the cigarettes will keep in an airtight container for up to 4 days. (Yield: about 24 cookies.) *

Continued on page 178

Variation: Chocolate-Filtered Cigarette Cookies

While the cookies are cooling, spread a sheet of parchment on a work surface. Melt 4 ounces of bittersweet chocolate in a small saucepan over simmering water, just until liquefied. Don't let the chocolate get hotter than 110°F. Remove from the heat, and allow to sit at room temperature, stirring occasionally. Dip one end of each cookie into the chocolate, coating about a fourth of the length. Place the coated cookies on the parchment to harden.

Sauces, Stocks,
and
Gifts from the Kitchen

Marinara Sauce

Linda Carucci

✳

This is a great sauce for Baked Stuffed Manicotti (recipe on page 90), for pasta, or for topping a pizza.
Make more than one batch, and store the leftover sauce in the refrigerator. It will keep for up to 3 days.

2 tablespoons olive oil

1 small onion, minced

¼ teaspoon dried leaf oregano,
minced

4 cups peeled, seeded, and diced tomatoes
(or canned tomatoes in puree)

1 teaspoon salt

¼ teaspoon freshly ground pepper

¼ teaspoon sugar

1 tablespoon chopped fresh Italian parsley

1 tablespoon chopped fresh basil

1. Heat a heavy 2-quart saucepan over medium heat. Add the olive oil. When the oil is hot, add the onion, and sauté until it just begins to brown. Crumble in the oregano, and stir.

2. Add the tomatoes, salt, pepper, sugar, and parsley, and bring to a boil. Reduce the heat, and simmer for 10 to 15 minutes, until the sauce is no longer watery. Adjust the salt and pepper, if necessary. When the sauce is cooked, stir in the basil. (Yield: 4½ cups.) ✳

Fresh Tomato Sauce

Lars Kronmark

❋

Remember new French cuisine and how fast it was gone again?
Well, a few things stayed behind, and this is one: fresh tomato flavor.

3 medium tomatoes

Salt to taste

Sugar to taste

Black pepper to taste

¾ cup virgin olive oil

¼ cup vinegar

6 fresh basil leaves,
finely chopped

1. Blanch the tomatoes in boiling water for 10 seconds, chill them in an ice bath, and remove their skins and seeds.

2. In a blender or food processor, puree the tomato flesh for about 5 seconds. Add the salt, sugar, and pepper.

3. With the machine running, slowly add the oil and vinegar, blending for 2 to 3 minutes to make a smooth mixture.

4. Pour into a bowl, and stir in the basil. (Yield: 1½ cups.) ✳

Mushroom-Thickened Sauce

Dan Bowe

❋

This flavorful sauce is ideal for pastas and as an accompaniment to or as
the base for a sauce for beef or hearty poultry, such as turkey.

2 cups Roasted Vegetable Stock
(recipe on page 185)

1½ cups chopped button mushrooms

¼ teaspoon dried (or ⅜ teaspoon fresh) basil

¼ teaspoon dried (or ⅜ teaspoon fresh) thyme

⅛ teaspoon dried rubbed sage

Salt and pepper to taste

1. Bring all the ingredients to a boil in a medium saucepan.

2. Reduce the heat, cover, and simmer for 20 to 30 minutes, or until the solids are very soft.

3. Strain the stock, reserving the solids.

4. Transfer the solids to a food processor or mini-chop, and process to a smooth puree, adding a bit of stock, if necessary.

5. Add the remaining stock to the processor, and pulse to combine.

6. Return the sauce to the saucepan, and heat just to a boil. Pour into a sauce bowl, and serve. The sauce can be stored in the refrigerator for up to 3 days. (Yield: 2 cups.) ✳

Variation: Fennel-Thickened Sauce

Omit the mushrooms, basil, thyme, and sage. Substitute ½ cup chopped fennel bulb, in ½-inch pieces; ¼ teaspoon toasted fennel seeds, lightly crushed; and a pinch of saffron. Use with a seafood pasta or chicken dishes.

Extracted Red Pepper Juice Sauce

Johnathan Robinette

Use this procedure to make all kinds of exciting extracted vegetable juice sauces. Yellow bell peppers, carrots, and beets are other vegetables that yield vibrantly colorful and very flavorful extracted juice sauces. Don't be afraid to experiment, and use the sauces to decorate the plates and enhance the flavors of some of your favorite dishes. These sauces are extremely versatile and work well with meat, seafood, and poultry.

3 red bell peppers,
seeded and cut into 1/2-inch strips

1/2 cup olive oil

1. Process the bell peppers in a juice extractor. (Reserve the pulp for a flavoring agent, if desired—see recipe on page 184.)

2. Transfer the juice into a saucepan, bring to a boil, and reduce the liquid by about half, until large bubbles form.

3. Pour the reduced juice into a bowl that is sitting in an ice bath, and let cool to room temperature.

4. When the juice has cooled, slowly drizzle the oil into the juice, whisking vigorously to incorporate it and form a temporary emulsion. (If the mixture is too dry to emulsify, add a few drops of cold water, and whisk again.)

5. Pour the sauce into a squeeze bottle. The sauce may be stored in the refrigerator for up to 2 months. (Yield: 3/4 cups.) *

Extracted Vegetable Pulp Flavoring Agents

Johnathan Robinette

✻

The pulp that collects in a juicer as a by-product of juicing vegetables is very flavorful. Most people don't know what to do with it, so they throw it away. Here is an excellent use for this pulp. You may combine several dried pulps to create exciting seasoning agents (see the recipe on page 82, for example).

Vegetable pulp

1. Heat the oven to 180°F. Line a cookie sheet with parchment paper.

2. Spread the vegetable pulp in a very thin, even layer on the cookie sheet, and bake for 6 hours, until the pulp is completely dried.

3. Crumble the pulp into a spice mill, and grind it into a coarse powder. Store in an airtight jar at room temperature until ready to use. It will keep for up to 6 months. ✳

Roasted Vegetable Stock

Dan Bowe

✻

Stock can be frozen in an ice cube tray to make small portions easy to defrost and use.
Be sure to label and date your stocks so you can tell how old they are.

1 medium red onion, quartered

2 medium yellow onions, quartered

6 cloves garlic

2 leeks, split lengthwise and cut
into 2-inch pieces

2 ribs celery,
cut into 3-inch pieces

2 carrots, unpeeled, rinsed, and cut
into 2-inch pieces

2 tomatoes, quartered

1/2 cup white wine

12 cups water

1 teaspoon fennel seed, toasted
and lightly crushed

2 teaspoons coriander seed, toasted
and lightly crushed

1 bay leaf

4 sprigs thyme

12 parsley stems

1/2 tablespoon salt

1 teaspoon black pepper

1. Heat the oven to 375°F.

2. Place the onions, garlic, leeks, celery, and carrots in a large oven-proof pan that can also be used on the stove (such as a roasting pan with handles or a large sauté pan). Roast for 30 minutes.

3. Add the tomatoes, and roast for 15 to 20 minutes more, until the vegetables are a dark golden brown but not burned.

4. Remove the pan from the oven, and deglaze it with the wine over high heat on the stovetop.

5. Place the mixture in a large stockpot, and add the remaining ingredients.

6. Bring to a boil, lower the heat, and simmer for 45 minutes (or 1 hour for a richer stock).

7. Remove from the heat, and cool in the pot on a rack.

8. Strain, and store for use later. Stock will keep in the refrigerator for up to 5 days and in the freezer for up to 2 months. (Yield: 3 quarts.) ✻

Variation: Light Vegetable Stock

Place all the ingredients in a large stockpot in the order listed. Proceed with steps 6–8 of the main recipe.

Basic Chicken Stock

Johnathan Robinette

Chicken stock is such a staple in professional kitchens that chefs always expect it to be there.
For home use, it's a good idea to make a large quantity, pour the stock into ice cube trays, and freeze it.
You can store the cubes in a self-seal bag in the freezer for up to 3 months.

2 bay leaves

10 parsley stems (no leaves)

1/2 teaspoon dried leaf thyme

12 to 14 whole black peppercorns

3 pounds chicken bones
(wings, backs, and necks)

2 large onions,
cut into 3/4-inch dice

2 large carrots,
cut into 3/4-inch dice

2 stalks celery,
cut into 3/4-inch dice

About 4 quarts cold water

1. Place the bay leaves, parsley stems, thyme, and peppercorns in a 6-inch square of cheesecloth. Gather up the corners, twist together, and tie the sachet closed with butcher's twine. Set aside.

2. Rinse the chicken bones well under cold running water. Place them in a heavy, 6-quart stockpot.

3. Add the onions, carrots, and celery, and pour in enough of the water to completely cover the bones. Drop in the herb sachet.

4. Bring to a boil, and skim any impurities that come to the surface.

5. Reduce the heat, and simmer, uncovered, for 2 to 3 hours, skimming impurities as necessary.

6. Line a strainer or china cap with several layers of dampened cheesecloth, and strain the stock through. Use a ladle or large spoon to gently press any remaining liquid through the strainer. Discard the bones, vegetables, and sachet.

7. Allow the strained stock to cool completely. Then transfer to an airtight container, and store until ready to use. The stock will keep in the refrigerator for up to 1 week and in the freezer for up to 3 months. (Yield: about 10 cups.) *

Basic Fish Stock

Johnathan Robinette

This stock uses an herb sachet to add flavor. Here it is strained out of the stock with the vegetables. In stews and other recipes where the sachet alone is removed before serving, tie the sachet closed using one end of a 12-inch-long string, so you can tie the other end to the handle of your pot. This makes the sachet easy to remove and discard.

2 bay leaves

8 parsley stems
(no leaves)

½ teaspoon dried thyme leaves

14 to 18 whole black peppercorns

2 pounds fish bones, tails,
and heads (gills removed)

1 tablespoon butter

1 small onion,
cut into ¼-inch dice

1 stalk celery,
cut into ¼-inch dice

½ cup dry white wine

7 to 8 cups cold water

1. Place the bay leaves, parsley stems, thyme, and peppercorns in a 6-inch square of cheesecloth. Gather up the corners, twist together, and tie the sachet closed with butcher's twine. Set aside.

2. Clean the fish bones thoroughly under running water.

3. Melt the butter in a heavy, 6-quart stockpot. When it is hot, add the onion and celery. Sweat the vegetables over medium heat, stirring occasionally, for 3 to 5 minutes, until the onion is translucent.

4. Place the fish bones on top of the vegetables, and cover with a piece of parchment paper. Reduce the heat to low, and sweat the bones for about 5 minutes, until they turn opaque. Remove and discard the parchment paper.

5. Add the wine, and bring to a simmer. Then add enough of the water to cover the bones completely, and drop in the herb sachet.

6. Simmer, uncovered, for 25 to 30 minutes, skimming any impurities from the surface.

7. Line a strainer or china cap with several layers of dampened cheesecloth, and strain the stock through. Use a ladle or large spoon to gently press any remaining liquid through the strainer. Discard the bones, vegetables, and sachet.

8. Allow the strained stock to cool completely. Then transfer to an airtight container, and store until ready to use. The stock will keep in the refrigerator for up to 1 week and in the freezer for up to 3 months. (Yield: about 6 cups.) *

Salsa Verde
(Roasted Tomatillo Salsa)

Tamara Frey

✳

This is one of many different kinds of salsas. Dried chilies and tomatoes are used
in some others. The classic *salsa Mexicana* is freshly minced tomato, onion, jalapeño, and
cilantro: red, white, and green, the colors of Mexico's flag.

½ pound tomatillos, husks removed

1 serrano chili (or jalapeño)

1 clove garlic, coarsely chopped

1 tablespoon chopped cilantro

1 tablespoon minced yellow (or white) onion

Salt to taste

1. Heat a dry sauté pan, and roast the tomatillos whole, along with the chili, over medium heat, covered, for 8 to 10 minutes, until soft and browned on the sides.

2. Remove the tomatillo mixture from the pan, and place in a mortar or a food processor, with the garlic, cilantro, and onion.

3. Grind or puree the salsa until it is slightly chunky (or the consistency you desire). Add the salt, and serve as a condiment. (Yield: 1½ cups.) ✳

Tomato-Ginger Chutney

Teresa Douglas / Mitchell

*Chutney is one of the most versatile foods around and a great way to use late harvest bounty.
The cooking time is lengthy, but so is the shelf life. I typically present it to friends as a host / hostess gift,
and it also makes a wecome addition to a gift basket.*

4 pounds plum tomatoes,
seeded and chopped

6 large cloves garlic,
minced

6 yellow onions,
thinly sliced

1/3 cup fresh ginger,
peeled and minced

1 cup dark raisins

1 cup golden raisins

1 cup white wine

1 1/2 cups brown sugar

1 1/2 cups red wine vinegar

1 teaspoon salt

1/2 teaspoon cayenne

1. Sterilize enough canning jars for 8 pints of chutney.

2. Mix all the ingredients in a large stainless steel pot. Simmer for about 2 hours, until the mixture is cooked through and most of the liquid has been absorbed.

3. Pour the chutney into the sterilized jars. Cover, and store at room temperature. The chutney will keep for several months. (Yield: 8 pints.) *

Herb-Flavored Vinegar

Teresa Douglas/Mitchell

✳

Herb vinegars are so simple to make and so impressive to receive! I scour antique shops and flea markets for unusual glass bottles that really show off the herb sprigs.

The most important thing to consider when making flavored vinegars is a good pairing of the vinegar and the herb. Delicately scented selections do very well with mild champagne vinegars, for example, and robust herbs with red wine vinegars.

1 cup fresh herbs (rosemary, tarragon, chives, thyme, sage, or oregano, or a combination)

3 cups mild vinegar

5 (or more) sprigs herbs
(same kind as used above)

1. Crush the 1 cup of fresh herbs, and place them in a covered jar with the vinegar. Steep for 1 month in a cool, dark place.

2. Strain through cheesecloth or a paper coffee filter. Bottle the vinegar with the sprigs of fresh herbs. ✳

Fruit-Flavored Vinegar

Teresa Douglas / Mitchell

✳

Fruit vinegars are perhaps one of the most rewarding food gifts. Although they are simple to make, they are not readily available commercially. Strained, bottled, and assembled, they create a display of delicate colors and can provide a focal point to salads and seafood dishes.

4 cups chopped fruit
(cranberries, raspberries, blueberries, blackberries, pears, or nectarines, or a combination)

2 cups champagne (or mild white or apple cider) vinegar

1. Place the fruit in a glass jar (or crock). Pour the vinegar over it.

2. Cover, and store at room temperature away from the light for 2 to 10 days. Strain through cheesecloth or a paper coffee filter until absolutely clear. ✳

Variation: Island-Fruit Vinegar

Use papaya, mango, or pineapple and rice wine vinegar.

Simple Syrup

California Culinary Academy

✳

3 cups sugar

1 cup corn syrup

3 cups water

1. Place the sugar in a large saucepan, and make a well in the center of it. Pour the corn syrup into the well. Then add the water, and bring the ingredients to a boil without stirring.

2. Boil for 3 to 5 minutes, until the sugar has dissolved completely. Skim any impurities that rise to the surface.

3. Remove from the heat, and cool to room temperature.

4. Pour the syrup into a bottle, and store, covered, at room temperature for up to a week or in the refrigerator for up to a month. (Yield: about 6 cups.) ✳

Fondant

California Culinary Academy

About 2½ cups cool water

2 cups confectioners' sugar

½ cup corn syrup

1. Place 2 cups of the water and the sugar in a medium saucepan, cover, and bring to a boil. Boil gently until the mixture reaches 230°F, removing the lid only to check the temperature.

2. Add the corn syrup, and continue to boil, uncovered, until the temperature reaches 238°F.

3. Oil a large marble surface. Pour the boiling mixture onto the marble, and immediately sprinkle enough of the remaining cool water on top to cover and cool the mixture, watching out for sputtering.

4. Allow the mixture to cool to room temperature. Then spread the fondant back and forth with a wide spatula (or metal scraper) to incorporate air into it, until it is smooth and white.

5. Store the fondant at room temperature, in an airtight container, with just enough water on top to keep it from forming a skin. It will keep for up to a month. (Yield: 2 cups.) ✳

Pastry Cream

Michael Kalanty

Pastry cream is a staple of the dessert kitchen. This version is thick enough to be used as a filling for cream puffs and fruit tarts, though it can also be lightened with whipped cream and served as a sauce (see Pastry Cream Mousseline Sauce on page 196).

3 cups milk

1 vanilla bean

1/8 teaspoon salt

1 1/4 cups sugar

8 egg yolks

3 tablespoons cornstarch

4 tablespoons plus 1 teaspoon flour

1. Pour the milk into a medium saucepan. Split and scrape the vanilla bean, and add it to the milk. Add the salt and half of the sugar. Scald the mixture, stirring occasionally.

2. In a small bowl, whisk the egg yolks with the other half of the sugar until the mixture reaches the ribbon stage (falling like a ribbon from the whisk). Add the cornstarch and flour, and beat to make a paste.

3. Gradually pour about half of the scalded milk mixture into the egg mixture, whisking gently to incorporate. Pour the egg mixture slowly into the remaining milk, whisking gently.

4. Return the mixture to the stove, and cook over low heat, stirring constantly with a wooden spoon for about 2 minutes, until the mixture thickens to the texture of heavy cream. Increase the heat to medium, and cook, stirring vigorously. Use a whisk briefly when small lumps form, then return to stirring with a wooden spoon. Increase the heat to medium–high, and continue to stir vigorously until the mixture comes to a boil. Cook, stirring constantly, for 1 1/2 minutes more.

5. Transfer the pastry cream to a stainless steel bowl, and place it in a larger bowl filled with ice water to cool. Stir occasionally.

6. When it is cool, cover the pastry cream with plastic wrap, and refrigerate it. It will keep for up to 3 days. Remove the vanilla bean before using. (Yield: 3 cups.) *

Pastry Cream Mousseline Sauce

Michael Kalanty

✳

The term *mousseline* indicates that a flavorful base preparation has been lightened through the addition of whipped egg whites or cream. In this case, a vanilla pastry cream is made more delicate by folding in whipped cream, creating an elegant sauce that pairs well with fruit (and other) desserts. This mousseline may be flavored with 2 tablespoons of liqueur or alcohol (such as Grand Marnier, cognac, or rum), folded into the pastry cream along with the whipped cream, to accent the flavors of the fruit.

1 cup heavy cream

1 tablespoon sugar

1/2 teaspoon vanilla extract

2 1/2 cups Pastry Cream
(recipe on page 195)

1. Whip the cream until soft peaks form. Add the sugar and vanilla, and whisk until firm peaks form.

2. Fold the whipped cream into the pastry cream.

3. Cover with plastic wrap, and refrigerate until ready to use. (Yield: about 4 cups.) ✳

Crème Fraîche

California Culinary Academy

✳

1 cup heavy cream

1 tablespoon buttermilk

1. Combine the ingredients, and allow to sit in a tightly covered jar at room temperature for 24 hours. Store, refrigerated, until ready to use. Crème fraîche will keep for up to 1 week. ✳

Vanilla Tulip Paste

Bo Friberg

1 cup (2 sticks) unsalted butter, softened

1 cup confectioners' sugar, sifted

1 cup egg whites, at room temperature

1 teaspoon vanilla extract

2$\frac{1}{3}$ cups cake flour, sifted

1. In a large bowl, cream the butter and confectioners' sugar together.

2. Incorporate the egg whites, a few at a time.

3. Add the vanilla extract.

4. Mix in the flour.

5. Store, covered, in the refrigerator, until ready to use. Tulip paste will keep for several weeks.

6. Allow the paste to reach room temperature, which will bring it to a spreadable consistency, before using. (Yield: about 4 cups.) ✳

Variation: Chocolate Tulip Paste

Omit the cake flour. In step 4, sift together 1$\frac{1}{2}$ cups bread flour and $\frac{1}{2}$ cup plus 1 tablespoon unsweetened cocoa powder, and incorporate them into the butter mixture. (Yield: about 4 cups.)

Champagne Chocolate Sauce

Teresa Douglas / Mitchell

✳

This sauce is so good on so many things that it doesn't last long. It really jazzes up premium ice cream, pound cake, or dessert tarts. It can also be made with a variety of liqueur substitutes instead of champagne, and it is wonderful just plain (without alcohol), the way they used to make it for drugstore soda fountains.

4 ounces semisweet chocolate

4 ounces bittersweet chocolate

1 cup heavy cream

¼ cup blush champagne
(leftover is fine)

⅓ cup sugar

1. Chop the chocolate into small chunks. Set aside.

2. In a heavy medium saucepan, warm the cream, champagne, and sugar over moderate heat until it is hot to the touch.

3. Remove the pan from the heat, and quickly whisk in the chocolate until it is melted. You can store the sauce in the refrigerator for up to 30 days. (Yield: 2½ cups.) ✳

Brandied Butterscotch Sauce

Teresa Douglas / Mitchell

This sauce looks beautiful in a decorative glass jar or bottle. It makes something
special of warm gingerbread, simple cakes, or nut tarts. I like to swirl it into
Champagne Chocolate Sauce (recipe on page 198) for a foolproof dessert plate garnish.

3 cups sugar

1 cup water

2 cups heavy cream

8 tablespoons (1 stick) butter

4 tablespoons brandy

1. Whisk the sugar and water together in a heavy medium saucepan. Bring to a boil, and cook over medium-high heat, without stirring, until the sugar is a deep brown. (Swirl the pan if the sugar is coloring unevenly.)

2. Remove the pan from the heat, and pour in the cream. Carefully swirl the pan to combine the ingredients. When the sauce stops bubbling, return it to the heat, and stir it with a metal spoon.

3. Bring the sauce to a boil again, add the butter, and remove the pan from the heat. Stir in the brandy. Store the sauce in the refrigerator. It will keep for up to 30 days. (Yield: 4 cups.) *

Variation: Nonfat Butterscotch Sauce

Use 3 cups sugar and ¾ cup water in step 1. Eliminate the rest of the ingredients and steps.

Soft Fruit Ratafia

Teresa Douglas / Mitchell

✳

Ratafias (flavored liqueurs) are really rewarding to make. The French use the locally distilled spirit marc and whatever fruit or berry is in season. I use brandy or a clear spirit like gin or vodka, depending on the color and delicacy of the fruit. It's fun to make several varieties and offer a selection of homemade liqueurs to guests after dinner.

1¼ pounds apricots, peaches, cherries, or berries

1 pint brandy (or gin or vodka)

1 cup sugar

½-inch stick cinnamon

4 cloves (optional)

¼ teaspoon ground mace, ground ginger, or ground coriander (optional)

1. Peel, pit, and quarter or slice the fruit, depending on the variety you are using.

2. Place all the ingredients in a bottling jar, close it tightly, and marinate at room temperature for at least a month. ✳

Variation: Dried Fruit Ratafia

1 pound prunes, dried cherries, or dried apricots

3 ¼-inch-thick crosswise slices orange peel

1 cinnamon stick

1¼ cups sugar

1 cup water

1 pint brandy (or marc or armagnac)

1. Fill a wide-mouthed bottling jar with the dried fruit. Add the orange peel and cinnamon.

2. In a small saucepan, boil the sugar and water together for 5 minutes to make a syrup. Cool.

3. Add the syrup to the jar (it should be a third to half full). Top with the brandy.

4. Close the jar tightly, and marinate at room temperature for at least a month. ✳

Sugar-Glazed Nuts

Teresa Douglas/Mitchell

✳

This recipe was given to me by the mother of one of my college roommates, and I have made glazed nuts during the holidays ever since. You can eliminate the sugar and make a savory version, using curry or Mexican spices (cumin, coriander, and chilies), for example. Everyone likes these nuts, and they make terrific gifts to pack and ship.

1/2 cup white wine (or water)

4 egg whites, lightly beaten

2 cups sugar

2 teaspoons salt

8 cups whole nuts
(see variations below)

3 teaspoons ground spices
(see variations below)

1. Heat the oven to 250°F. Spray a cookie sheet with a nonstick spray.

2. In a large bowl, combine the wine, egg whites, sugar, and salt. Whisk until blended.

3. Add the nuts and spices. Toss to coat the nuts thoroughly.

4. Spread the nuts on the cookie sheet. Bake for about 1 hour, until browned and dry. Stir occasionally to prevent sticking.

5. Cool the nuts, and store them at room temperature in an airtight container. (Yield: 8 cups.) ✳

Variation: Cinnamon Almonds

Use 8 cups roasted almonds and 3 teaspoons ground cinnamon.

Variation: Gingered Pecans

Use 8 cups pecan halves, 2 teaspoons ground cinnamon, and 1 teaspoon ground ginger.

Variation: Five-Spice Walnuts

Use 8 cups walnut halves, 1 teaspoon ground cinnamon, 1 teaspoon ground nutmeg, 1/4 teaspoon ground cloves, 1/4 teaspoon ground allspice, and 1/2 teaspoon ground ginger.

Glossary

AA sugar: A large-grained sugar used for decoration on baked goods. Also known as decorators' sugar.

al dente: Literally "to the tooth." The degree of doneness at which cooked vegetables and pastas have a slight bit of resistance to them when chewed. The vegetables are cooked yet crisp, and the pastas are still slightly firm, not mushy.

arugula: A green leaf lettuce with a subtle peppery flavor when young and a hot mustardlike flavor when mature. Also known as rocket, Italian cress, and rugola.

Asiago cheese: A semifirm cheese that melts very well and is often used grated. For grating, the cheese should be at room temperature.

bain-marie: A container for food placed into (or over) a container filled with simmering water, to cook the food gently. Also known as a water bath.

bâtard: An oblong loaf of bread shorter and thicker than a baguette.

buffalo mozzarella: Mozzarella cheese made from buffalo milk.

Bundt pan: A deep tube pan with sides that curve and are indented, producing a cake with an attractive sculptured exterior. The center tube allows for even cooking and shapes the cake into a ring.

butter (verb): To spread a thin even layer of butter on the interior surface of a pan.

butterfly (verb): To slice in half across the thickness (of a shrimp or chicken breast, for example) without completely cutting through, so that the halves can be spread open like a book.

Calvados: A spirit distilled from cider.

caramelize (verb): To brown sugar by cooking it to between 320°F and 360°F.

carne asada: Meat that is already cooked. Usually an inexpensive cut of meat is used, and it is roasted.

carpaccio: A dish composed usually of raw beef sliced very thinly and decorated with colorful sauces and garnishes. Named for an Italian artist whose work was wildly colorful.

challah: A style of egg bread that is traditionally served on the Jewish Sabbath.

chanterelle mushroom: A small, yellow mushroom with a frilly edge.

Chantilly cream: Whipped cream that is sweetened, usually with confectioners' sugar.

chiffonade: A preparation technique in which leafy greens, such as fresh herbs or lettuces, are cut into thin strips or shreds of varying thickness, resembling the flowing texture of chiffon fabric.

chile de árbol: A small, thin hot pepper closely related to the cayenne and Thai peppers. It may be purchased green, red, or dried.

china cap: A cone-shaped, fine-meshed strainer with a handle, usually made out of metal. Also known as a chinois.

chipotle chili: A jalapeño pepper that has been smoke-dried.

clarified butter: Butter from which the milk solids and water have been removed, leaving pure butterfat, which has a higher smoking point and less butter flavor than unclarified butter.

cloves (of garlic): The small, individual sections of a bulb of garlic.

coppa colla: A cured meat usually available in Italian delicatessens.

crème fraîche: A slightly tart, thickened cream,

similar to sour cream, made by curdling cream. It cannot be made with ultrapasteurized cream, which does not contain enough bacteria to curdle.

crepe: A thin, delicate, unleavened pancake used to wrap fillings in both sweet and savory dishes.

cut in (verb): To mix a solid fat (butter, solid vegetable shortening, or lard, or a combination) and dry ingredients (flour plus salt, baking powder, baking soda, and/or sugar) with a cutting motion and utensil.

deglaze: To swirl a small amount of liquid in a pan over moderate heat to dissolve cooked particles and caramelized drippings that remain on the bottom after sautéing or roasting.

devein (verb): To remove the dark line of digestive tract running along the back of a shrimp or prawn.

dice (verb): To cut food into small cubes.

dock (verb): To prick a dough, usually with a fork, so that steam will escape during baking and the dough will not rise.

egg wash: A mixture of egg (yolk and/or white) beaten (often with a pinch of salt) and generally thinned with water or milk. It is used to give a shine to baked items or as an adhesive (for example, to seal the edges of ravioli together).

fish fumet: A fish stock. In professional kitchens it is called *fumet* to preclude confusion with any other stock, because if you use a fish stock instead of a chicken stock, for example, the results can be very unpleasant.

five-spice powder: A spice used often in Asian cuisine that consists of star anise, anise seeds, cloves, cinnamon or cassia, and Szechwan peppercorns ground to a powder.

flambé (verb): To ignite liquor added to a food.

flash (verb): To place food under a broiler or in a very hot oven, either to melt cheese, to caramelize the surface, or to reheat quickly.

flour (verb): To dust a surface or the inside of a pan lightly with flour to prevent food from sticking to it.

fold in (verb): To incorporate a lighter substance into a heavier substance with a turning motion that mixes from top to bottom.

frangipane: A sweet almond and egg filling.

ganache: Chocolate enriched with cream and sometimes also flavored with liquor.

grissini: An Italian bread stick made with Parmesan cheese.

guajillo chili: A mild variety of chili pepper that may be either green or red.

habanero chili: A very hot variety of chili pepper, generally the size of an apricot, that turns from green to red as it ripens. Also known as Scotch Bonnet.

hard ball stage: A stage in the boiling of sugar syrup, registering 257°F to 275°F on a candy thermometer, at which a small amount dropped into cold water can be rolled between the fingers into a firm ball. At this point the syrup is still clear and has not picked up any color.

hard crack stage: A stage in the boiling of sugar syrup, registering 293°F to 302°F on a candy thermometer, at which a small amount dropped into cold water shatters into hard, brittle threads.

herbes de Provence: A combination of herbs typically found in the Provence region of France, consisting of lavender, savory, thyme, chervil, and sage.

hoisin sauce: A Chinese sauce made from fermented soybeans that may also contain flour, sugar, and garlic.

julienne (verb): To cut an ingredient (usually a vegetable) into sticks about 1/8 by 1/8 by 1 to 2 inches.

mascarpone: A soft-textured cheese, similar to cream cheese, that is slightly sweetened.

mesclun: A type of leafy salad green.

mille-feuilles: Literally "1,000 leaves." A pastry dough made with many layers, so that it is light and flaky. It is a version of puff pastry but does not have as many layers as a traditional puff pastry.

mince (verb): To cut into small dice or pieces, usually less than ⅛ inch.

miso: Fermented soybean paste, used to flavor soups and other dishes.

mortadella: An Italian-style pork sausage larded with cubes of fat and black peppercorns.

mousseline sauce: A sauce or cream lightened by folding in whipped cream. Also a delicately flavored combination of ground white meat (poultry, pork, or veal), fish, or shellfish lightened with cream and egg whites.

oil (verb): To coat the interior surface of a pan with an even layer of oil.

pancetta: An unsmoked, peppered bacon.

parchment paper: Nonwaxed, moisture- and heat-resistant baking paper, sold in sheets or rolls, that is used to line pans, to wrap foods for cooking, and for many other purposes.

parcook (verb): To cook partially.

pâte brisée: A dough that produces a very flaky crust for pies and other dishes.

petite sirah: A wine made from petite sirah grapes primarily associated with the Rhône Valley in France but also produced in the United States and other countries.

pinch: An imprecise unit of measurement, usually less than ⅛ teaspoon. For a pastry pinch, the thumb and forefinger only are used; for other items, the middle and third fingers may also be used.

pizza stone: A ceramic tile that is heated in the oven and used for baking breads and pizza. The dough is placed directly on the stone.

proof (verb): To allow yeast in a dough to grow and give off carbon dioxide, causing the dough to rise.

phyllo: A wheat flour dough that is rolled into tissue-thin sheets and sold frozen in packages. Also spelled *filo*.

radicchio: A variety of lettuce, often red and white in color, with a slightly bitter flavor.

ramekin: Any baking dish designed for a single serving.

rapid-rise yeast: A baking yeast with a nutrient added to aid the yeast in creating carbon dioxide.

reduce (verb): To cook a liquid mixture so that some of the water evaporates, intensifying the flavors.

ribbon stage: A stage at which ingredients (typically eggs and sugar) that are beaten together reach a thick consistency that forms a ribbonlike design when dropped from a spoon or poured slowly.

roast garlic (verb): To bake a whole, unpeeled bulb of garlic in an oven until the cloves have softened to a puree and caramelized.

roast peppers (verb): To heat peppers either in the oven or directly over a flame until the skin is charred.

roulade: A slice of meat, fish poultry, or other ingredient that is rolled around a filling. Also a filled and rolled sponge cake.

roux: Equal parts (by weight) of flour and fat (usually butter) that are cooked together. It is typically used as a thickening agent.

Sambuca: An Italian distilled liquor made from witch elderberry bush and other ingredients, with a distinctive anise flavor.

sauté (verb): To cook raw ingredients quickly in a small amount of fat in a large, flat-bottomed pan. It comes from the French word *sauter,* which means "to jump." In sautéing, you pull the pan toward you with a rapid, jerking motion. The food catches on the far lip of the pan, "jumps" in the air, and falls back into the pan turned over to cook on another side.

Sauternes: A sweet wine made in a region in France from a combination of sauvignon blanc and sémillon grapes. It should not be confused with sauterne, a semidry white American wine.

scald (verb): To heat to 180°F to 190°F, just below the boiling point.

sear (verb): To brown food (usually meat) quickly over high heat to seal in the juices.

set: Baked until the yolks of an egg mixture have cooked and the mixture is not runny.

shiitake mushroom: A medium to large, flat mushroom with a slightly smoky flavor. The stem is tough and generally must be trimmed away. Also known as Black Forest mushroom.

simmer (verb): To cook food by submerging it in a liquid that is kept just below boiling, usually between 170°F and 180°F.

soft peaks: A stage in beating an ingredient (such as egg whites or cream) at which the ingredient forms a droopy but definite peak when the beater is lifted from the bowl.

sorbet: A flavored ice that is churned during the freezing stage. It has a smoother texture and a higher sugar content than a *granité*.

soufflé dish (or cup): An ovenproof round dish (or ramekin) with straight sides and a flat bottom.

stiff peaks: A stage in beating an ingredient (such as egg whites or cream) at which the ingredient forms peaks that hold their shape and do not droop when the beater is lifted from the bowl, and the mass does not slide when the bowl is tipped.

strudel: A dessert (or savory dish) in which a paper-thin flaky dough encases a filling.

sucanat: An organic cane sugar.

sweat (verb): To cook a raw ingredient (usually a vegetable) in a small amount of fat over low to medium heat without caramelizing or browning the ingredient, until it softens and releases moisture.

taleggio cheese: A quick-ripening, soft cheese similar to brie.

temper (verb): To combine two ingredients with different temperatures by adding small amounts of the hotter ingredient to the cooler one, so that their temperatures are more balanced before they are folded together.

tomatillo: A fruit native to Mexico that resembles a green tomato, although the two are only distantly related. (Both are in the nightshade family, but the tomatillo is more closely related to the cape gooseberry.) It is encased in a papery husk, which must be removed before the fruit is used.

torpedo onion: A very sweet Bermuda onion shaped like a football or torpedo.

wasabi powder: The powder used to make wasabi paste, the very hot green "mustard" typically served in Japanese restaurants.

zest: The colored, outermost layer of the skin of citrus fruits. It contains essential oils that carry the flavor and aroma of the fruit.

Nutritional Analysis per Serving

✳

	Calories	Carbohydrate (g)	Protein (g)	Fat (g)	Cholesterol (mg)	Sodium (mg)
Afternoon Tea Sandwiches	322	29	10	18	52	475
Antipasto Platter	761	75	38	36	72	1740
Apple Pie with Crème Fraîche and Black Pepper	586	75	5	29	83	97
Apple-Potato Galettes with Goat Cheese	457	35	14	31	66	585
Artichoke and Mushroom Risotto with Asiago Cheese and Sun-Dried Tomatoes	533	69	12	20	30	832
Baby Pumpkin Salad	320	24	5	24	5	372
Baked Santa Barbara Shrimp	779	19	27	67	193	543
Baked Stuffed Manicotti	384	18	22	25	200	519
Brie and Arugula Open-Faced Sandwiches	243	18	9	14	30	374
Browned Butter Cigarette Cookies	252	34	3	12	31	29
Bruschetta with Mushrooms and Smoked Provolone	668	46	25	41	43	1353
Cappuccino Mousse with Sambuca Cream in a Chocolate Cup	761	56	9	59	261	74
Caramelized Onion and White Cheddar Soufflé with Stout	384	19	15	28	317	877
Carne Asada and Chili Calzone	2325	201	88	131	197	1876
Champagne-Chocolate-Chestnut Torte	438	51	5	25	128	111
Chicken Breasts Stuffed with Taleggio Cheese, Prosciutto, and Sage	824	22	51	61	137	638
Chile Toreado con Camarones (Hot Chilies with Prawns)	133	11	12	3	73	177
Chilled Mochaccino Pie	612	62	10	37	305	121
Chocolate Ganache Cake	794	71	12	53	296	83
Cioppino	322	9	37	8	135	361
Cold Cucumber-Lime Soup	92	15	7	1	4	131
Cornmeal Pound Cake	229	29	3	12	72	58
Country Cassoulet	645	112	27	13	0	1078
Cranberry-Chestnut-Turkey Sausage Patties	179	3	20	9	87	286
Crème Caramel Nouvelle	597	116	11	11	233	129
Crêpes à la Bretagne	278	44	3	11	30	154

	Calories	Carbohydrate (g)	Protein (g)	Fat (g)	Cholesterol (mg)	Sodium (mg)
Crostini with Herbed Goat Cheese and Marinated Sun-Dried Tomatoes	993	44	14	89	22	516
Crostini with Kalamata Olive Tapenade	666	22	8	63	9	1432
Crystallized Ginger Biscotti	165	23	2	7	42	129
Curried Pumpkin Soup with Chutney Cream	199	35	9	4	3	328
Danish Bear Claws	909	81	15	62	143	303
Danish Raisin Snails	324	49	4	14	51	149
Flaming Rum Bananas with Meringue	228	45	5	2	3	48
Focaccia	416	48	8	22	0	553
Fresh and Dried Fruit Compote	193	35	1	0	0	7
Frozen Chocolate Soufflé (*Soufflé Glacé*)	518	39	8	42	188	58
Fruit and Cream Scones	349	49	4	16	56	337
Fruit Baskets	357	49	8	15	204	56
Galette of Potato and Celery Root	442	40	7	29	58	467
Giant Fruit Popover	606	90	12	23	213	527
Gravlax on Rye Bread with Mustard-Dill Sauce	236	19	20	8	55	1004
Grilled *Chipotle*-Citrus Quail	423	42	32	14	0	1053
Grilled Monkfish Medallions with Fennel-Olive-Tomato-Lemon Relish	247	3	21	17	39	357
Grilled Seasonal Vegetables with Aioli	800	25	8	78	106	154
Individual Passion Fruit Soufflés	248	54	4	3	7	92
Italian Frittata with Artichoke Hearts and Roasted Red Onions	383	22	24	23	539	403
Leek and Anaheim Chili Custard with Chili Salsa and *Habanero* Cornbread	629	83	19	24	288	698
Lemon Curd Parfait	918	64	9	72	438	353
Lemon Wafers	113	20	2	3	8	73
Marinated Five-Pepper Salad with Buffalo Mozzarella	368	13	15	28	53	711
Marmalade Muffins with Streusel	216	32	4	8	24	162
Mexfest Crepes	635	46	27	40	224	1230
Mille-Feuilles with Seasonal Fruit	493	49	8	30	112	169
Orange Soufflés with Grand Marnier	96	18	4	0	0	47
Oven-Roasted Home Fries	147	28	3	3	0	424
Palmiers	153	20	2	7	12	51
Pasticiotti	628	71	12	33	126	146

	Calories	Carbohydrate (g)	Protein (g)	Fat (g)	Cholesterol (mg)	Sodium (mg)
Peaches Poached in Sauternes with Mascarpone	226	29	2	13	39	19
Pear Frangipane Galette	505	74	6	22	87	81
Persimmon-Walnut Cake	623	77	9	33	112	152
Pesto Tarts with Glazed Leeks and Smoked Salmon	408	53	12	17	8	510
Plain Omelet	337	2	19	28	671	189
Pork Tenderloin with Mango and Four-Pepper Sauce	517	25	25	36	137	571
Raspberry Tea Tarts	191	17	4	12	12	234
Raspberry-Cassis Sorbet	125	26	1	0	0	9
Red Snapper Basil Ragout	489	43	29	22	42	382
Ricotta Crepe Soufflés with Fresh Raspberry Sauce	506	68	17	19	131	275
Roasted *Guajillo* and Garlic Chowder with Rosemary Sourdough Croutons	256	45	9	6	9	107
Roasted Vegetable Bread Pudding	277	26	11	15	138	429
Sacristains	350	35	5	22	27	123
Santa Fe Chili-Cheese Roll-Ins	590	83	20	20	67	396
Sautéed Sea Bass with Red Bell Pepper, Yellow Onion, and Thyme Seasoning	250	5	43	6	93	156
Seared Ahi Tuna with Sesame Seed and Black Peppercorn Crust on Asian Salad	582	36	74	16	128	756
Smoked Swordfish Carpaccio	321	31	16	14	21	946
Soufflé Roulade	456	7	15	41	228	330
Spiced Pear Cobbler	749	138	8	21	54	1082
Spinach and Corn Strudel	755	35	17	65	52	460
Steamed Mussels and Clams	437	10	24	31	61	405
Sticky Bun Pull-Aparts	820	141	14	25	74	488
Summer Brochettes with Orange-Ginger Marinade over Quinoa Pilaf	776	130	31	11	86	1216
Tabbouleh in Grape Leaves	189	20	3	12	0	537
Thai Chicken Pizza	756	101	25	27	17	1303
Tomato and Red Onion Salad with Goat Cheese	226	16	9	16	22	200
Trout in Grape Leaves with Apple-Grape-Mint Relish	449	13	42	20	115	852
Vanilla Shortbread	239	23	2	16	41	101
White Chocolate and Pistachio Bavarian with Chocolate Lace	618	69	7	36	41	71
Wild Rice and Potato Pancakes with Field Greens in Mustard Vinaigrette	821	109	19	34	127	922

Recipes Featured in Each Show

✳

Festive Favorites includes recipes only referred to by chefs in Cooking at the Academy and some variations not mentioned in the series, as well as the featured recipes listed below.

Cooking with Cheese

Brie and Arugula Open-Faced Sandwiches, page 28
Fresh Mozzarella, page 50
Marinated Five-Pepper Salad with Buffalo Mozzarella, page 52
Chicken Breasts Stuffed with Taleggio Cheese, Prosciutto, and Sage, page 65; Marinara Sauce, page 180
Pasticiotti, page 134

Cooking with Chilies

Roasted *Guajillo* and Garlic Chowder with Rosemary Sourdough Croutons, page 57
Leek and Anaheim Chili Custard with Chili Salsa and *Habanero* Cornbread, page 92
Chile Toreado con Camarones (Hot Chilies with Prawns), page 72

Cooking with Grains

Tabbouleh in Grape Leaves, page 43
Artichoke and Mushroom Risotto with Asiago Cheese and Sun-Dried Tomatoes, page 98; Light Vegetable Stock, page 185
Wild Rice and Potato Pancakes with Field Greens in Mustard Vinaigrette, page 42; Crème Fraîche, page 196

Danish and Breakfast Sweets

Fruit and Cream Scones, page 4
Danish Dough, page 7; Danish Raisin Snails, page 9; Danish Cinnamon Rolls, page 10; Danish Bear Claws, page 11; Bear Claw Filling, page 12; Simple Syrup, page 193; Fondant, page 194; Pastry Cream, page 195
Sticky Bun Pull-Aparts, page 3

Delicious Pies

Pâte Brisée, page 127
Apple Pie with Crème Fraîche and Black Pepper, page 131
Chilled Mochaccino Pie, page 132

Easy-to-Make Soufflés

Caramelized Onion and White Cheddar Soufflé with Stout, page 94
Soufflé Roulade, page 96; Extracted Red Pepper Juice Sauce, page 183
Individual Passion Fruit Soufflés, page 146

Egg Cookery

Plain Omelet, page 18
Omelet with Fresh Fruit, page 20
Italian Frittata with Artichoke Hearts and Roasted Red Onions, page 16

Entertaining on a Budget

Spinach and Corn Strudel, page 34; Fresh Tomato Sauce, page 181
Red Snapper Basil Ragout, page 81
Pork Tenderloin with Mango and Four-Pepper Sauce, page 62

Entertaining with Crepes

Basic Crepes, page 143; Buckwheat Crepes, page 143
Crêpes à la Bretagne, page 144
Mexfest Crepes, page 74
Ricotta Crepe Soufflés with Fresh Raspberry Sauce, page 145

Fancy Cookies

Palmiers, page 174
Sacristains, page 176
Browned Butter Cigarette Cookies, page 177; Chocolate-Filtered Cigarette Cookies, page 178
Crystallized Ginger Biscotti, page 171

Festive Salads

Tomato and Red Onion Salad with Goat Cheese, page 47
Baby Pumpkin Salad, page 51; Smoked Bacon Vinaigrette, page 51
Smoked Swordfish Carpaccio, page 44; Smoked Swordfish, page 44; *Grissini*, page 110

Fresh and Saltwater Fish

Seared Ahi Tuna with Sesame Seed and Black Peppercorn Crust on Asian Salad, page 86
Grilled Monkfish Medallions with Fennel-Olive-Tomato-Lemon Relish, page 84
Trout in Grape Leaves with Apple-Grape-Mint Relish, page 85

Gifts from the Kitchen

Herb-Flavored Vinegar, page 190; Fruit-Flavored Vinegar, page 192
Sugar-Glazed Nuts, page 201
Tomato-Ginger Chutney, page 189
Vanilla Shortbread, page 173; Chocolate Shortbread, page 173
Champagne Chocolate Sauce, page 198
Brandied Butterscotch Sauce, page 199

Healthful Entertaining

Pesto Tarts with Glazed Leeks and Smoked Salmon, page 30
Summer Brochettes with Orange-Ginger Marinade over Quinoa Pilaf, page 68
Orange Soufflés with Grand Marnier, page 153
Cold Cucumber-Lime Soup, page 59

About the California Culinary Academy

Mission Statement

We are leaders and innovators in the culinary industry. We research, develop, and provide professional quality education, information, products, and services to our students, the foodservice industry, and the consumer marketplace. Our objective is to create and enhance the ultimate culinary experience for our customers.

The California Culinary Academy was founded in San Francisco in 1977 as a professional school for chef training. One of the largest culinary schools in the western United States, the Academy is situated near the heart of downtown San Francisco, a city internationally acclaimed for its world-class dining establishments. With more than 3,000 restaurants, the city provides ample employment and learning opportunities for students and graduates. The Academy's proximity to several wine-producing regions allows it to offer special courses, tastings, field trips, and food and wine pairing contests to take advantage of this unique opportunity.

The Academy has 13 professional kitchen laboratories for practical training, a fully equipped culinary theater, and ample classroom space. Additional learning facilities include two student-staffed restaurants, which are open to the general public five days a week for lunch and dinner, and a retail shop featuring a variety of food products prepared by students as well as a wide array of cookbooks and culinary-related merchandise.

The California Culinary Academy, a publicly held company traded on the NASDAQ National Market System, strongly believes its for-profit orientation creates a real-world learning environment, which prepares graduates to meet the needs of the foodservice industry.

Career Training Programs

The California Culinary Academy offers two professional education programs: a 16-month professional chef training program leading to an Associate of Occupational Studies (AOS) degree in culinary arts, and a 30-week certificate program in baking and pastry arts. These programs, which combine theory, practical training, and hands-on experience, are designed to prepare students for employment opportunities in the foodservice industry. An educational advisory committee, including leading industry figures Julia Child, Bert Cutino, André Fournier, Robert Mondavi, Richard Swig, and Martin Yan, offers ongoing advice and guidance for these programs.

The 16-month AOS degree program includes hands-on cooking classes, as well as instruction in food and beverage management that emphasizes all phases of kitchen management, wine and food affinities, and table service. The training qualifies graduates for careers in cooking, dining service, restaurant management, and ownership.

The 30-week professional baking and pastry program is patterned after the same intense learning experience provided in the 16-month program. Aspiring bakers and pastry chefs learn the baking procedures, techniques, and presentation skills necessary for success in today's modern baking operations.

The Academy is recognized for its postsecondary educational program by the U.S. Department of Education and by the California Council for Private Postsecondary and Vocational Education. The California Culinary Academy is accredited by the Accrediting Commission of Career Schools and Colleges of Technology, and its culinary arts degree and baking and pastry programs are accredited by the American Culinary Federation Educational Institute Accrediting Commission.

The Profession

The foodservice industry, the nation's second largest employer, is one of the fastest growing industries in the United States. The U.S. Bureau of Labor Statistics projects an increase in demand for trained culinarians in excess of 30 percent over the next decade, which outpaces the projected growth of the total labor pool during that same time period. This growth translates into more than two million new career opportunities in the foodservice industry. Graduates of the Academy have been especially successful in developing careers based on their specific areas of interest in the culinary arts. The vast majority of our graduates are placed directly into foodservice positions after graduation.

Whether you are seeking a career in a traditional restaurant setting, wish to open your own restaurant or catering business, or want to pursue one of the many culinary career alternatives from food styling and photography to product research and development, the California Culinary Academy will help you reach your goal.

Restaurants

The California Culinary Academy has two full-service, student-staffed restaurants and three private dining rooms, which are open to the public Monday through Friday for lunch and dinner. These facilities are also available for banquets and special events during the week and on weekends. The Carême Room offers the finest in contemporary cuisine, while the award-winning Academy Grill presents a grill-style menu in a casual setting.

To learn more about the California Culinary Academy's educational programs or for restaurant reservations:

Telephone toll-free from outside San Francisco:
1-800-BAY-CHEF (1-800-229-2433)

Telephone from within the San Francisco Bay Area:
415-771-3536

Consumer Education

In addition to its professional education programs, the California Culinary Academy reaches out to cooking and wine enthusiasts through its consumer education program. Classes appropriate for all interests and ability levels cover everything from basic cooking techniques to fancy desserts, ethnic cuisines, and wine tasting/pairing classes. The Academy also develops custom classes and team-building events for companies and private groups. There are even classes for young cooking enthusiasts, including Culinary College for Kids and a similar program for teens. Classes are conducted at the San Francisco campus and, beginning in 1995, at the Academy's two culinary centers at The Broadway department store in Costa Mesa, California, and Broadway Home Dome in Las Vegas, Nevada.

CALIFORNIA
CULINARY
ACADEMY

Producer's Acknowledgments

Making a television cooking series depends upon the harmonious collaboration of many people. From chefs and food stylists to editors and engineers, dozens of talented individuals contribute in a spirit of culinary camaraderie to bring a series to fruition.

A production such as *Cooking at the Academy* also depends on the support and generosity of the community at large – in a real sense, the same kind of support that has become the foundation of public television itself.

For their generosity and kind support, special thanks go to our funders and to those individuals and companies who donated their time, talent, food, furnishings, and equipment in support of the second season of *Cooking at the Academy.*

To the entire production team listed below–those dedicated men and women whose expertise and professionalism are evident in each program–I extend my heartfelt thanks. Working with you has been a pleasure.

Production Staff

Peter L. Stein	*Executive Producer*
Bruce Franchini	*Director*
June Ouellette	*Associate Producer*
Tina Salter	*Associate Producer*
Kate Zilavy	*Assistant to Producer*
Joanne Sutro	*Director of Production Marketing*
Carl Abbott	*Chef / Kitchen Manager*
Greg Swartz	*Operations Manager*
Jolee Hoyt	*Unit Manager*
Ron Haake	*Set Designer*
Greg King	*Lighting Director*
Steve Siegelman	*Writer*
Denise Vivaldo	*Food and Prop Stylist*
Terence Ranger	*Makeup and Hair*
Andrew Lewis	*Assistant Food Stylist*

Kitchen Staff

Cristine Swett	*Kitchen Staff*
B. Chuck Fong	*Kitchen Staff*
Sarah Kennedy	*Kitchen Staff*
Michele Royston	*Kitchen Support*
Jack Ervin	*Kitchen Support*
Robin Basdeo	*Kitchen Support*

California Culinary Academy

Alexander M. Hehmeyer	*President / CEO*
David Chomsky	*Co-Executive Producer*
Jurgen Weise, CMC	*Technical Advisor*

Studio / Post-Production Staff

Walt Bjerke	*Studio Supervisor*
Dick Tally	*Studio Supervisor*
Greg Overton	*Camera Operator*
Harry Betancourt	*Camera Operator*
Eric Shackelford	*TD / Video*
Laurie Simms	*VTR Operator*
djovida	*Audio*
Nancy Bellen	*Editor*
Jon Herbst	*Editor*
John Andreini	*CMX Editor*
Dick Schiller	*CMX Editor*
Helen Silvani	*CMX Editor*
Margaret Clarke	*Stage Manager*
Randy Brase	*Stage Manager*
Jim Summers	*Stage Manager*
Eric Dauster	*Manager, Engineering Operations*
Larry Reid	*TV Operations*
Sylvia Mullally-Aguirre	*Narrator*

Our Talented Chefs

Dan Bowe, Linda Carucci, Tamara Frey, Bo Friberg, Louie Jocson, Michael Kalanty, Lars Kronmark, Teresa Douglas / Mitchell, and Greg Tompkins

LINDA BRANDT
Series Producer
San Francisco, 1995

Cooking at the Academy thanks the following companies for their generous support of the second season's programs.

✳

Food provided by:

BiRite Foodservice Distributors
Straus Family Creamery

Equipment and props for the series and the photographs in this book provided by:

Accurate Appliance
B.I.A. Cordon Bleu, Inc.
Bernardaud
Braun Inc.
Chicago Metallic
Corning Consumer Products Company
Everpure, Inc.
Heritage House, San Francisco
Johnson-Rose Corporation
San Francisco Marriott
Circulon Commercial
Oscartielle Equipment, California
Packard Fine China
Pier 1 Imports
Rosenthal China & Crystal
Russell Range, Inc.
Thomas by Rosenthal
Villeroy & Boch
Wedgwood USA, Inc.
Wüsthof-Trident Trading Company

California Culinary Academy Acknowledgments

The success of the first season of *Cooking at the Academy* and development of the second season have been made possible through the joint vision and dedication of many people at both California Culinary Academy, Inc. and KQED, Inc. First and foremost, I'd like to thank my fellow board members of the California Culinary Academy for their individual and collective support: Theodore Crocker, Chairman of the Board; William DeMar; and Robert Marani. William DeMar was especially instrumental in garnering crucial underwriter support for this project. Thank you, Bill, for your dedication to the vision.

Thank you to David Armanasco and Cindy Railing of Armanasco Public Relations, Inc. for their continued professional insight and dedication to the Academy and this series. Their efforts to bring the first season of *Cooking at the Academy* to the attention of the media and the foodservice industry were integral to its success. As we embark on the next season, their talents continue to add value to the project. They are important members of the California Culinary Academy and *Cooking at the Academy* teams.

A special thank you to David Chomsky, director of the Academy's media division, who also served as co-executive producer for the series. He was a key member of the team that developed the concept for this season of *Cooking at the Academy* and wrote scripts for several of the episodes. The fact that Mr. Chomsky is a graduate of the California Culinary Academy is an additional source of pride for us all.

Thanks to Chefs Jurgen Weise, CMC, and Johnathan Robinette who served as technical directors for the program. One of only 68 Certified Master Chefs in the United States, Chef Weise spent countless hours on the set during filming to ensure that every aspect of the show met the highest professional standards, while Chef Robinette provided technical expertise throughout development of recipes for the programs. Their attention to detail and comprehensive culinary knowledge show in each frame, resulting in a product that represents the educational quality standards for which the California Culinary Academy is known.

Thank you to all of the Academy chef/instructors who provided professional consultation, recipe development, and support for this project and especially to those full-time chef/instructors who hosted programs: Bo Friberg, Michael Kalanty, and Lars Kronmark. This season, the cast of *Cooking at the Academy* was extended to include some of our talented alumni; thank you to Dan Bowe, Linda Carucci, Tamara Frey, Louie Jocson, Teresa Douglas/Mitchell, and Greg Tompkins. Thank you also to Academy alumna Denise Vivaldi, who was the food stylist for the series. Chefs Carucci, Tompkins, and Vivaldi are also members of the Academy's adjunct faculty.

Thanks to all of the students at the Academy who have supported the series. Most particularly, I'd like to recognize several students who gave tirelessly of their time and talents to make this project a success. Thank you to Andrew Lewis, Jack Erving, Michelle Royston, Robindra Nauth Basdeo, Christine Wolf, Catherine Kinney, and Catherine Beckert, culinary stars of tomorrow.

Special thanks to Kristina Colangelo, my executive administrative assistant, who has coordinated various aspects of this project in the same flawless manner that is her trademark. Always organized, insightful, calm, and unflappable, she keeps everything running smoothly.

Thank you to each member of the KQED team who, once again, demonstrated why KQED is the nation's leading public television producer of cooking programs: Joanne Sutro, Peter Stein, Linda Brandt, Bruce Franchini, and Pamela Byers.

Finally, I wish to extend a personal thank you to the companies who have provided the underwriting support that has made this production possible: Meyer Cookware; Wüsthof-Trident; Everpure, Inc. and their distributor Water, Inc.; and Chicago Metallic.

ALEXANDER M. HEHMEYER
President and CEO
California Culinary Academy, Inc.

Index

✻

Page numbers in *italic* designate the photograph of the dish.

Page numbers in *italic* designate the photograph of the dish.

Page numbers in *italic* designate the photograph of the dish.

Page numbers in *italic* designate the photograph of the dish.

O

oil, herbed, 114
olives
    black, on antipasto platter, 48
    green, on antipasto platter, 48
    Kalamata
    in relish, 84
    tapenade of, for *crostini*, 26
    and walnut focaccia, 114
omelet
    cheese, 18
    with fresh fruit, *19*, 20
    plain, 18
onion, red
    for brochettes, 68
    in chutney cream, 54
    in frittata, 16
    and tomato salad, 47
    in vegetable stock, 185
onion sprouts, 86
orange juice, 66, 68
oranges
    in compote, 126
    individual soufflés, 153

P

palmiers, 174, *175*
pancakes
    wild rice and potato, with field greens
        in mustard vinaigrette, 40, *41*
    see also galettes
pancetta, with monkfish, 84
papaya, vinegar flavored with, 192
papaya nectar, in sauce, 62
parsley, in tabbouleh, 43
passion fruit, soufflés, 146
pastaciotti, 134
paste, tulip
    chocolate, 197
        for ribbon sponge cake, 122
    vanilla, 197
        for baskets, 160
        for cookie butterflies, 124
        for cookie spoons, 157
        for pirouette cookies, 140
pastry cream, 195
    in bear claws, 12
    mousseline sauce, 196
pastry dough. *See* dough

pâte brisée (flaky pie dough), 127
    for apple pie, 131
    for mochaccino pie, 132
    for pear galette, 128
peaches
    poached in Sauternes, with
        mascarpone, 166
    ratafia, 200
peanut
    butter, in torte, 118
    sauce (Thai), on pizza, 71
pears
    cobbler of spiced, 164
    dried, 14
    tart of, 128
    vinegar flavored with, 192
pecans
    glazed, ginger, 201
    in sticky buns, 2
pectin powder, 148
pepper, black, with apple pie, 131
peppercorns, black, 86, 166
peppers. *See* bell pepper/s; chili
persimmon and walnut cake, 119
pesto, tomato, 32
pie
    apple, with crème fraîche and black
        pepper, 131
    chilled mochaccino, 132
    custard, 132
    potato and celery root, 100
pilaf, quinoa, 70
pineapple
    for mille-feuilles, 170
    vinegar flavored with, 192
pine nuts, in pesto, 32
pistachio nuts, and white chocolate
    Bavarian, 148
pizza, Thai chicken, 71
pomegranate seeds, 56, 126
popover, giant fruit, 14
pork
    ground, in sausage patties, 21
    tenderloin, with mango and four-pepper
        sauce, 62, *63*
potatoes
    baking (russet)
        in galette (pie) with celery root, 100
        for galettes (cakes), 36
        individual soufflés in, 95
        and wild rice pancakes, 40
    in cassoulet, 88

potatoes (*continued*)
    focaccia, 114
    new, 88
        see also potatoes, red
    red (new)
        oven-roasted home fries of, 22
        in ragout, 81
    rosefir, 88
    white, in chowder, 57
    yellow fin, 88
prosciutto
    on antipasto platter, 48
    in soufflé, 95
    in stuffed chicken breast, 65
provolone
    on antipasto platter, 48
    smoked, 27, 48
prunes, 4, 200
pull-aparts, sticky bun, 2
pumpkin
    salad of baby, 51
    soup of curried, with chutney cream,
        54, *55*
    and walnut cake, 119
pumpkin seeds, toasted, 51

Q

quail, grilled *chipotle*-citrus, 66, *67*
queso fresco, 92
quinoa, pilaf, 70

R

ragout, red snapper basil, 81
raisins
    in chutney, 189
    in Danish snails, 9
    golden, 126, 189
    in scones, 4
raspberry/ies
    in baskets, 160, *161*
    and cassis sorbet, 168, *169*
    for chocolate Bavarian, 148
    with peaches, 166
    sauce, 145, 163
    in tea tartlets, 136
ratafia (fruit liqueur), to make, 200
relish
    apple-grape-mint, 85
    fennel-olive-tomato-lemon, 84

Page numbers in *italic* designate the photograph of the dish.

Page numbers in *italic* designate the photograph of the dish.

Page numbers in *italic* designate the photograph of the dish.